JIMMY MAC THE MEDIUM

Carrie Roberts

Jimmy Mac the Medium Copyright © 2018 by Carrie Roberts. All Rights Reserved.

All rights reserved. No part of this book may be reproduced in any form or by any electronic or mechanical means including information storage and retrieval systems, without permission in writing from the author. The only exception is by a reviewer, who may quote short excerpts in a review.

Proofed by Kate Collingwood

Events, locales and conversations have been recreated from memory. And the stories of Jimmy's childhood are told from his perspective. In order to maintain people's anonymity names of individuals and places have all been changed. I may have also changed identifying characteristics and details such as physical properties and occupations to protect the privacy of individuals.

ISBN-13 978-1-7950430-1-4

This book is dedicated to my beloved husband and wonderful daughter without whose help, encouragement and support this book would never have been completed

Carrie Roberts

PREFACE

I was compelled to write this book after listening to Jimmy's funny and scary stories. Jimmy makes a very curious, interesting, and emotional read. His story brings together his unique and touching experiences as a medium, whilst also drawing on the devastating impact of depression. It's the story of Jimmy growing up in a poor family in the North East of England. Being both funny and sad, it's about discovering his psychic abilities and the problems he faced with mental health difficulties. Along the way there have been many frightening and scary encounters. He endured the horror of finding his father's body on holiday in Greece – and at one point he became homeless living on the streets due to depression. All these hardships have created stronger empathy and understanding, turning him into the robust person and gifted Medium he is today.

♦ ♦ ♦

Carrie Roberts

MEDIUMSHIP

Many people do not know what Mediumship is and are frightened just by the thought of speaking to dead people. They often have preconceived ideas of what happens during a spiritual encounter, so I will try to explain what Mediumship is and how it works. When a person is a Medium it simply means they have an ability that allows communication between people who are alive and others who have died. Normally, it is a natural gift that an individual will discover during the course of their life. Some people have this capability from being a young child, whereas other people may develop it later in life. My gift came and went while I was growing up, but each time it returned it was getting stronger.

To me being a Medium is second nature, but some people say they don't know what to make of me when we first meet. For instance, one friend explained the initial time we met a black cloud appeared to be hanging over my head. She didn't know if it was because I had a sad or depressing life, or if I was evil. This lady was a Catholic; she found out about me being a Medium so assumed the latter and was scared in my presence. This was because she had never experienced seeing something like this before - especially, as she put it, 'since I was dabbling in the occult.' My now friend, Linda, was perturbed and found it disturbing that she could see this ominous cloud surrounding me, particularly as I was communicating with the dead as this is strictly forbidden in the Catholic faith.

However, as we knew the same people, we couldn't help but be introduced and talk to each other. Linda soon discovered that I wasn't evil but downhearted. When I was in a good mood, she said the cloud lifted and was replaced by a much brighter countenance with the odd sparkle even. But the black cloud returned when I sank into my unhappy state. She also realised, by my actions and words that I tried to be supportive and help people so wasn't a malevolent or evil person like she first imagined.

It transpired that her only other experience of anything comparable to this was in church, where she sometimes saw what she described as halos around peoples' heads. She noticed this when they were on the altar and presumed, they must be very holy. Later in her life, she realised the 'halos' were part of the energy bodies belonging to the people she saw and nothing to do with being holy. This made a lot more sense to her once she understood the idea of energy. She observed that the people surrounded by halos didn't seem to be particularly holy once they were outside church living their normal day-to-day lives.

Generally, people think mediums can look up to Heaven and contact any spirit they want but the best way to explain the concept is that a medium serves like a radio receiver tuning into information from another world or dimension. A light switches on when their channels of communication are open, so they can be spotted easily in the alternate dimension, or what people understand and articulate as the 'spirit world.' Seeing this light, the 'spirits' know where they can go to pass on any advice to be relayed to the relatives of the deceased. This voice is powerful. It usually brings comfort to the family and friends, putting their minds at rest. Finally, they can understand their loved ones are happy and in a safe place.

Any spirit who notices the light will approach. For protection, spirit guides are present to ensure any bad spirits don't get through. This is a totally different situation to when uninformed people innocently meddle with the spirit world. For instance, when playing with

Ouija boards and asking, 'Is there anybody there?' you are asking any passing spirit to enter. They are invited where ever they are from or whatever they did when they were alive. Never would you consider a situation whereby you open your front door on a dark night, advertising your vulnerability with a bright flashing neon sign to attract and welcome those passing by into your house. This would certainly be a mistake. Under no circumstances would you welcome thieves or murderers into your home in the physical world; the spiritual world is no exception.

Mediums are not in control of who they speak to or what these spirits want to offer. A person wanting to receive a message from a particular loved one or an answer to a question cannot be guaranteed to converse with the relative they want unless the departed person actually wants to come and speak to them. If a person came wanting to contact Great Aunt Gertrude to find out where the family treasure is hidden, the medium cannot page Gertrude and request her presence - she can only be spoken to if she comes of her own accord. More often than not if there is a large audience, I can see a crowd of spirits waiting to speak to me, and it's the ones who want to pass a message on most strongly to their family members that tend to get through first.

Connections with the spirit world bring understanding and peace at concerning times. On one Friday evening I visited friends Paul and Carrie to have a catch up. We spent a pleasant evening together when a mutual friend Ian, who had died of kidney failure, came to visit and pass a message on for my friends: *'you may think you are going to die - but don't worry, you will be fine everything will be alright.'* Paul and Carrie didn't really pay much attention to the message. They didn't know what it meant. They humoured me saying, "yes okay" in a way that was equivalent to giving me a pat on the back. On the Sunday of the same weekend, Paul began having continuous palpitations. These didn't stop and he felt quite unwell.

Having visited the out of hour's hospital that night, he saw a German Doctor who had been flown in to cover for the weekend. Valium was prescribed for Paul, who was told by the doctor he was suffering from stress and should rest at home. Faint and no better Monday morning, Paul visited his own GP who performed an ECG scan. Immediately rushed to hospital following the results, Paul was fearful. It came as quite a shock to both Paul and Carrie that this was a serious problem that required such urgency. When you experience a heart problem, terrifying thoughts flood your mind.

Mortality is suddenly something you begin to contemplate.

During the ambulance ride, Carrie was struck by her memory of Ian's message. *You think you are going to die but everything will be okay.* She now understood the significance of Ian's communication.

Relief washed over Carrie as she exhaled breathing a sigh of relief. Waiting in the hospital coffee lounge she was able to leave her worries with the staff attending to Paul's condition. Without receiving Ian's message, she would have been fraught, frantic and frightened. Carrie told me she would have panicked, being 'anxious and worried to death' about what was happening but was able to remain calm. Thanks to the contact from Ian, she was in a lot more control of her emotions.

Paul was very lucky. His particular condition was diagnosed, meaning it could be treated successfully and his heart rate slowly returned back to its normal rhythm. Sent home with emergency medication, Paul was prepared should it happen again. While being treated, Ian's reassuring words also played a soothing role in Paul's mind. He knew he was going to be fine.

Messages from the 'other side' can bring great comfort to individuals. In this case, not only did the message ease Paul's worry, but it also prevented Carrie from having a total meltdown. Ian's words calmed an alarming time of distress.

There are different forms of Mediumship: *clairvoyance* is the ability to see, *clairaudience* is the ability to hear and *clairsentience* is the ability to sense or feel the presence of spirits. Mediums have varying abilities; some may use only one of these methods whereas others may use more. I use all three.

My name is Jimmy Mac, and here is my story relating to how my skills developed and various instances throughout my life that have made my abilities stronger. My account tells of my family life, relationships, mental health problems, and how my experiences have moulded me into the medium I am today.

♦ ♦ ♦

MY BACKGROUND

Born in 1963 into a poor family in Stockton-on-Tees in the North East of England, my earliest recollections were of Mam and Dad arguing all the time. They would shout, scream and bellow at each other at the tops of their voices and it would go on for ages. It seemed like an eternity to us kids shut in another room out of the way. Eventually, it would always end in the same manner with Dad leaving the house slamming the door behind him shouting, 'I'm going back to the pub.'

My brother and sister and I would listen silently until the fighting stopped. It was inevitable how it would conclude with Dad storming out and Mam shouting obscenities down the road after him. Mam would come back in ranting and raving; she would then get all dolled up and disappear off out somewhere. She would leave without the slightest thought for her kids or what we might be doing.

My twin brother Patrick shared a room with me. We had to sleep in the same bed from necessity because of lack of space and lack of money. The room we slept in was downstairs close to the front door so we could always hear when our parents had a fight. They always seemed to be fighting. We heard many arguments although we didn't really understand what they were all about, but it was obvious that Mam and Dad didn't get on.

In a way it was quite good when they had an argument. It meant that after they left to go to the pub, or wherever it was they went, we would have the entire house to ourselves, allowing us to get up to all sorts of tricks. We wouldn't always know where Mam disappeared to, but she always returned before Dad. She would always seem a lot happier since she would often sing at the top of her voice upon her arrival back home.

One thing was certain: we would always make sure we were in bed before our parents return so we wouldn't get in any bother from them. Somehow most nights we managed to time it dead right and make it back to bed just in the nick of time. First, we'd hear Mam roll in. She would bang about, singing incoherently, and Dad would turn up shortly after.

It was always easier to make sure we were in bed when they arrived home. If we were still up, the closest child got a kick up the backside before scarpering out of the way. Generally, we could run rings round them because of the states they were in; but they were like elephants who didn't forget, so the next day we knew at some point we would get a swift clip or kick for making a fool out of them.

◆ ◆ ◆

GROWING UP

This constant fighting was a normality of life which we had to tolerate but as we were used to it we just ignored the regular squabbling thinking it was common behaviour. We got on with our lives. However, this disorderly conduct was continuously in the background and probably affected the way we children behaved. As a young child I can mostly remember getting into a lot of scrapes with my brother Patrick. Most days, especially in the holidays, we would regularly be chucked out on the street first thing. As soon as we had downed something for breakfast, normally a piece of dry stale bread, we were unceremoniously ousted out the door. If we were very lucky, we were given an old lemonade bottle full of water, but no food and told to stay away till teatime. There we were for the rest of the day, bored with no money and nothing to do except hang around the streets. We didn't even have a ball, so we mainly used to get up to some sort of mischief to occupy the long days.

One day Patrick and I broke into the cricket club in Thornaby. We were about eight or nine years old and snuck into the club when nobody was about, but the only thing we could find were a few crates of Babysham. We decided to pinch them anyway and dragged them to the nearest bus stop, where, thinking it was like lemonade, we downed as many bottles as we could (which wasn't many at our age).

It didn't take us long to realise it wasn't like lemonade at all by how ill it began to make us feel, as a short time later we were starting to feel dizzy and sick, so we abruptly stopped guzzling our surreptitious booze. We felt so bad that we just wanted to go home no matter what the consequences were going to be when we got there, although we were soon to find out the result of our little excursion.

Arriving home, the moment we entered the house Mam instantly knew that we had been drinking. She had seen our Dad drunk often enough and she could easily read the signs. It wasn't difficult to make us confess what we'd been up to; she grabbed one of us by the collar and the other by the ear and we spilt the beans very quickly after that before both collapsing in a heap.

Sprawled on the floor thinking we'd got off easy without getting a good hiding, we were beginning to snigger; mouthing that wasn't as bad as we thought to each other. A minute later I could see the silhouette of my mother stood in the doorway of the kitchen. She was heading towards us at speed with determination in her stride, carrying something that was difficult to make out. A split second later I realised what was about to happen, but it was too late to save myself.

There in her hands was a red bucket filled with water, dripping as it was full to overflowing. Without a moment's hesitation this huge pail of ice-cold water was flung all over us as we laid prostrate on the floor. The shock made us both gasp for breath and sit up. Then the onslaught began.

The next thing I knew she was yelling at the top of her voice shouting a few good choice words and slapping us, all at the same time. Instead of making us return the bottles that were left and apologise to the club, she dragged us up off the floor by the scruff of the neck and sent us packing with strict orders to bring the remainder of the booze back home.

After being drenched there was a brief moment of respite as we were kicked back out of the house onto the street. There we breathed a sigh of relief and momentarily relished our getaway from the noise and chastisement. The relief only lasted a few seconds though, since we soon realised we were dripping wet and somehow had to get back to the bus stop. We shrugged in despair and hoped no one else had taken the Babysham; both of us were freezing cold and soaking but managed to drag ourselves back to our spoils, swaying and stumbling in a very sorry old state.

It must have taken a while but finally we got there, grabbed hold of the crates as best we could and dragged them home - shivering, constantly tripping and falling over. The crates felt a lot heavier than they did when we were sober, and we were very lucky that none of the loot got smashed.

Finally, after what seemed like a mammoth struggle we did get back to the house where Mam made us yank the crates through into the kitchen, giving us a slap for making a mess in the process. We were made to scrub the yard as punishment while she finished off the last few bottles of Babysham sat on the front doorstep.

Secretly, I think she was quite pleased with us for the free drink and she was in a good humour for the rest of the day. It was a shame we felt so ill and couldn't fully take advantage of her happy mood. Later on, I heard her telling one of her friends that she sent 'the little buggers' back to the bus stop to collect the crates so she could have a good drink, and even better than that it was completely free.

On the sly we were very proud of our little venture as it seemed to be the cause of a few days of Mam being in an especially good frame of mind.

◆ ◆ ◆

FAMILY LIFE

In those days men still worked long and hard; many of them hardly saw their kids, when they eventually did arrive home they were there just to discipline the children. It was the same for my Dad - he worked very hard long hours and when he had finished his shift, he would go directly to the pub to try and relax a bit before returning to the house. Payday was different however, because that day he made a beeline straight home, and would hand the majority of his money over to Mam for the housekeeping. Although, he always kept a bit back for himself to fund his drinking habit. Unsurprisingly this wasn't enough attention for Mam - she wasn't happy, and she must have been very lonely as Dad was always out. When he did come back, he always stank of beer and fags and never talked to anyone as he immediately fell asleep the moment he sat down in his chair. Subsequently, Mam had started to see other men and was having affairs.

The three of us kids were used to seeing Mam with other men, but never thought anything about it, as we were only young. These men never seemed to be around for long, but they were the reason why there were so many massive arguments. The fights were all about my mother's various male acquaintances. Eventually, and quite predictably, my parents split up. Mam couldn't take the loneliness any longer and dad was sick of being made a fool of by her and her men friends. So, one day Dad finally left the family home without really explaining what was going on.

As you can imagine I was extremely upset. This was a bolt from the blue. I thought my Dad was gone for good and I would never see him again and was left with an ache in my heart. My Mam didn't explain things either, and even though she could see how upset we all were she seemed happier. She didn't waste any time though, before she moved her current male acquaintance in. As when we woke up a day or so later, we discovered another man with three kids in our house. It was as if it was totally normal and they had always lived there. The man grunted as we walked in wide eyed, and the other kids barely noticed us, but Mam had a smile on her face; and most unusually, presented us with cereal for breakfast, which we ate, dumbfounded.

The bloke that had assumed Dad's place was a rag and bone man by profession, called Graham. I now had also acquired two stepsisters and a stepbrother John, all living in the two-up-two-down house. This made it quite hard for me - I felt like I'd lost my Dad, and my home had been invaded by people who I didn't know and didn't want in the house. Although, after a period of time and getting to know my new family; it was quite enjoyable having more sisters and another brother around. Soon I realised we still got to see my Dad as often as we wanted, and so we settled down into this new style of family life.

My stepdad Graham would supply the clothes for all six children from the rag and bone cart which saved him a lot of money. He had collected a great number of clothes from our neighbours and from other people in the local area, and everyone in the vicinity knew us and where we lived. My new brother and sisters still went to their old school where they got on okay. But Patrick, my sister and I went to a different school where we were known as the 'scruffy macca's' (our surname being MacCann). All the other kids knew our new dad was the rag and bone man; they would make fun of our clothes and call us names. The most likely reason there was so much amusement about our outfits was that we were probably wearing their old unwanted clothes they had thrown away for the rag and bone collection. As far as I was aware all the people in the neighbourhood and the kids at school suspected the Scruffy Macca's were wearing their cast-offs.

♦ ♦ ♦

MY ENCOUNTER WITH SPIRIT LIGHTS

John, my new stepbrother, had moved into the small downstairs room which I shared with my twin brother Patrick, making it very cramped. It was here in bed one night that unbeknown to me I had my first encounter with spirit in the form of beautiful flashing lights that surrounded me. At the time I thought I was imagining things, but the lights made me feel safe and comfortable and I drifted off to sleep watching them.

Another night asleep in bed - I was still only young but can't remember my exact age. It was three or four o'clock in the morning when something suddenly woke me up. Startled, I lay there for a bit feeling frightened but not knowing why, I could sense things were a bit off somehow, and had a feeling that there was something under the bed. Both of my brothers were fast asleep, and I didn't dare move or breathe, in case whatever it was I was sensing became aware of me attracted by my movement. Not even wanting to blink, I lay under the covers as still as possible. My eyes were wide, peeping out from under the blanket and staring intently into the dark trying to see or discover what was troubling me.

Filled with fear and covered in sweat, my pyjamas clung to me like a second skin. I was trying to hold my breath, so it couldn't hear me. The thoughts spinning through my mind were that there was a presence hiding in the shadows, and if I moved or caught its attention it would grab me, making me disappear never to be seen again. In my head all I had to do was remain perfectly still and silent to survive this ordeal.

Suddenly, my attention honed in on some movement on the floor. A spider of giant proportions had crept out from under the bed, and the glow from the night lamp made it cast a huge shadow creating the illusion it was the size of a cat. It stood in the middle of the floor seeming to challenge me, I stared, terrified, and could now hear my breath coming in short rasps. Closing my eyes as tight as possible, I wished the spider far away.

Eventually plucking up the courage and opening my eyes slightly, I squinted in the direction of the spider. It was still there but its manifestation felt even more ominous as it had moved closer to me. It didn't give the impression of being a normal spider; apart from its enormous size it emitted a menacing aura. For a second time my eyes snapped tightly shut as again the spider was wished as far away from me as it could possibly get. Again, I looked, and it moved silently and stealthily nearer than before. At that moment as my heart was pounding and my mouth was so dry my tongue was stuck to the roof of my mouth, something else caught my attention at the side of my head. I felt a sudden lurch as my stomach dropped with the fear and dread, the spider had a companion.

Not daring to move a muscle and keeping my head motionless, I slowly turned my eyes sideways as far as humanly possible. I got a great surprise as a flashing light had appeared on my pillow. Recognizing the twinkle of my comforting lights I suddenly felt calm. The panic within me dissipated as I wondered where this bright little twinkling ball of radiance had appeared from. Then to my amazement more and more sparkling lights came into focus. The harder I stared the more came into view surrounding me.

Completely forgetting about the spider, I sat gazing in wonder thinking how lovely all the little lights were and my body completely relaxed. They brought me reassurance and protection, and the room was bursting with lights – they were everywhere, all different colours, all sparkling and flashing. Feeling extremely happy I seemed to sink into my bed but felt as though I was floating at the same time.

In the middle of enjoying this lovely uplifting and soothing experience, an image of the spider abruptly popped into my head, but my thoughts had risen above feeling scared, When I looked, the spider had disappeared. This was the second time the lights had become visible to me - I especially liked not only the way they had managed to instantly dissolve my fears, but also the comfort that came with them.

◆ ◆ ◆

CHILDHOOD DEVELOPMENT

Soon after my encounter with the spider, my experiences became a bit strange. I'd started to become aware that I seemed to know things that were going to happen and had gut feelings about how situations would turn out. However, these glimpses of future events always seemed to be sad goings-on, and I never had any thoughts of anything good that might occur. For instance, going to meet my stepdads' Mam for the first time, I felt very uneasy and unhappy and didn't want to go. There was an unreasonable feeling of fear deep inside the pit of my stomach, but I had no idea why and got this constant nagging thought which urged me to stay away from this woman for some reason.

Nevertheless, the choice wasn't mine to make, and on arrival at my stepgran's house I was very wary. Although she seemed really nice and friendly, I felt a push to stay away from her; I had a feeling that told me not to get too close, and this was accompanied by a deep feeling of unease. However, I dropped my guard after a while and started having some fun in the garden, jumping around playing somersaults and handstands and eventually my new Gran called me over. She began with the pretence of tidying me up, tucking my shirt in my trousers but that's not all she did.

In addition, she began to feel down my trousers inside my pants and have a fiddle about, and then after a few minutes she let me go. Shocked and upset about what had just happened I didn't dare tell anyone what had gone on, but now understood the feelings were a warning. Any similar future feelings like that needed great attention paying to them and would require an awareness of anything happening around me in order to keep me safe.

Approaching the age of about ten years old I began to see colours emanating around people, and they were all quite different. Some were brighter than others, and some were quite dull; they could be multi coloured or just a couple of predominant colours. These, I now know, are commonly referred to as auras or sometimes the light body.

Observing the myriad of colours gave me a lot of pleasure, but I thought that everyone could see them so never really mentioned them to anyone. It was funny but it soon became apparent, even at my young age, that the people with a bright colourful aura were well-liked individuals who behaved in friendly helpful ways. There were also some people with dark gloomy auras, and I learnt to keep away from them as the majority weren't nice.

There was one man in particular who regularly came into contact with me as I often had to pass him in the street. This frightened me, and it didn't help that he was one of the people with a horrible murky looking aura. Passing him in the narrow part of the street one day, he kicked me for no reason. So, in the future, I kept away from him and would always walk on the other side of the road when I spotted him in the distance.

This experience taught me to keep well out of the way from anybody with muddy shades in the aura surrounding their body for my own benefit. After a while this particular aspect faded without me even really noticing; I remembered about the colours one day and realised they were no longer visible to me.

As a matter of interest, I think many children are capable of seeing auras before their gift is generally closed down unintentionally by people who don't understand it. For instance, remember the kids at school who used to paint the cows a different colour like red or blue. I have never thought about the colour of a cow's aura until today, but I remember Danny, a boy in class who had done just that. He had painted red cows in a green field, and the teacher kept saying, "the cows are black and white not red, why have you painted them red?"

He replied, "the cows are red," but she insisted he had to colour them properly and made him re-do the painting with black and white cows. So, you can see why seeing something differently doesn't work in our society because the grown-ups probably don't comprehend or have any concept of such things.

Danny may have been seeing the aura of the cow, or he could have been seeing red as the complementary colour of the green grass appearing on the mainly white bodies of the cows. Red is the opposite of green on the colour spectrum: if you stare at a green piece of paper on a white background for a minute or two and then remove the green paper still staring at the white, you will see red, and vice versa.

If you try this, you will be able to see colours similar to how they can appear in an aura. Try this little party trick with any colour you like, and if you stare long enough the opposite colour of the spectrum will appear. Interestingly enough, that's why doctors and nurses in the theatre wear green because it helps if they have been staring at blood during an operation for any length of time: when they look up, they can see green, but if people are wearing green, they don't notice so much.

Children on the whole are very open to being able to see unseen things that adults have lost the ability to perceive, as children are very intuitive. This reminds me of a time when one of my friends was having a problem with his daughter, Katie, aged two. Each night she would wake up crying and said that a man with a gruff voice and a funny face was talking to her. She couldn't understand what he was trying to say, but she didn't like it. My friend Colin posed this problem to me and asked what could be done, so I explained it could be a relative coming to visit to see his new family members. All Colin had to do was to explain to the visitor that he was upsetting Katie and ask him to please leave her alone.

So, the next night, when Katie began to complain, my friend went into her bedroom and asked her what the problem was. She said the man with the gruff voice is back and explained, "he is stood there," pointing to the end of the bed. Colin looked in the direction she had indicated and said, "Look, can't you see you are frightening Katie? Please leave her alone." Colin waited for a minute or two, and then Katie said the man had gone. She settled down. Following the incident, she slept peacefully that night and each subsequent evening after that, never mentioning the man again. My advice had solved the problem.

As a child my Mam also experienced spooky stuff and thought she was psychic. My Great Gran was actually a spiritualist. This was before the war and my Great Gran would hold services or secret meetings in peoples garden sheds, because in those days, spiritualism was frowned upon and so had to be performed furtively.

My Gran would hide or try and sneak in to these meetings if they were nearby when she was a child, and she would also try and read the tealeaves as she had watched her mother do. This gift was passed onto my mother who also liked reading the tea leaves. Perhaps this is where my psychic skills come from but growing up my own experiences of seeing colours and knowing things seemed to fade without me really being aware that they had gone.

I had too much going on in my life to pay attention to my innermost feelings. All I wanted to do was to leave school and start earning some money, but the tumultuous things that happened to me during my childhood probably kick started my psychic development.

♦ ♦ ♦

A DAY OUT AT SALTBURN

During my childhood I can clearly remember various incidents that happened to me where I should have been able to use my gift but wasn't able to call on it for some reason. Our day trip to Saltburn was one of those times. Dad would pick up his kids to see them every Sunday without fail, and one particular Sunday the weather was gorgeous, so he decided to take us to Saltburn for the day. At the time I must have been about ten years old.

Saltburn is a peaceful little Victorian Resort with a few old pubs on the seafront. It holds a special place in my heart as I've had many good times and have lots of memories there. It's a picturesque place brimming with history and tales of smugglers. There is a high cliff that towers over the sandy beach called Huntcliff where it is particularly easy to get cut off by the tide. Many tourists or even locals not paying enough attention have to be rescued as people get stranded at the bottom of the cliff when the sea comes in. It also has a pier and what is called a funicular, which is an old Victorian sort of cable car that runs up the side of the cliff. There are amusements on the pier and there used to be old-fashioned swing boats to play in.

Bearing in mind what a dangerous place Saltburn can be for adults, never mind unaccompanied children, Dad dropped us off on the seafront and said, "go and play I won't be long I've just got somewhere to go," and promptly disappeared. We started to play on the beach, while, unbeknown to us, Dad had gone back home to Stockton for his customary pub lunch. In the meantime, we weren't bothered that we couldn't see Dad anywhere as we were playing happily in the sand. For a long while, it was great fun on the beach. There is a stream that runs into the sea. We called it the red river because of its colour, as it can turn red on occasion from the iron ore in the old mines. On this particular day it happened to be red and we kept trying to jump over the stream, but it was too wide. We kept falling in and we all ended up soaked to the skin.

The sun was strong, and we began to turn red with sunburn, but we thought it was because we had been doused in the water so many times, we were turning red or rusty. Dad had gone to the pub and left us with no money, food or drinks, and we soon realised we were sore and starving, so started looking all over and shouting for our Dad. I often relied on my feelings of knowing about different things to help me navigate life and although we couldn't find him at first, I relied on my intuition. It was difficult to concentrate on our situation as my stomach was rumbling so much, although there was a certainty entering my gut that everything would be fine. Thanks to this feeling I wasn't really worried by Dad's disappearance, but I was so hungry.

We hunted high and low, searching everywhere we could think to look, but couldn't find him and with no money; we couldn't buy anything to eat or drink. So, using our initiative, we started trying to scrounge money or food off people, but no one would entertain us. Inevitably we went back to playing in the sand again to try and take our minds off our hunger pangs. This idea didn't last long as we were so tired and hungry, we didn't even have the energy to play. Consequently, we sat on a wall next to the bin of the food kiosk, hoping to eat a few left-over scraps people had thrown away. We waited with anticipation for our Dads return.

Meanwhile, back in Stockton, Dad had gone home after his lunch in the pub, and as usual had fallen asleep in his chair, completely forgetting about his kids who he'd left in Saltburn. He was awoken by my Grandad knocking on the door; he had decided to call round on the off chance we were in. Grandad made a comment that he thought my father was supposed to be looking after the kids today. Then realisation dawned on Dad of what he had actually done. Grandad told us later that he had never seen anyone in his state move so fast. He heard him shout 'bloody hell!' and then he was off out the door like a rat up a drainpipe. He jumped into his wagon and raced back along the roads to Saltburn to find his kids dirty, wet, red with sunburn and starving. We remember it as quite an adventure since most of the day we had good fun. I still love Saltburn and visit as often as I can.

♦ ♦ ♦

MOVING STORY

These sorts of incidents littered my childhood, but one day a very unusual thing happened to my twin brother Patrick and me. It was a Wednesday when we returned home from school as normal; it was just like any other day apart from the fact that we were sporting scuffed knees and muddy clothes from fighting on the field. On the way back, we thought we were going to be in bother, so decided we would try and sneak in to clean ourselves up a bit before we got caught. When we got there, we were messing about so much that we totally forgot our plan and went straight into the house as usual. The problem was that on entering, there was absolutely nothing inside the house. It was totally empty. Everything had gone. Imagine how we felt we were in total disbelief; there wasn't a stick of furniture, or cup or spoon, or anything to be found in any of the cupboards or rooms throughout the house. There was utterly and absolutely nothing left - not a scrap. The place was completely bare.

We stood and stared at each other, and then Patrick said that we must have gone into the wrong house. We both ran back outside to make sure we were in the right place – or the right street, even. When we confirmed in our minds that it certainly was our house, we fell over each other trying to squash back in through the front door together at the same time. We ran from end to end of the house, shouting and yelling for our mother, hoping for some explanation, but there was no reply. Our voices emanated a hollow, eerie echo as we ran shouting all the way through the house again, searching frantically for some clue as to what might have happened. We were screaming 'Mam' at the tops of our voices, but all we got in return was the sound of our yells echoing back at us, and then silence.

We were scared and frightened. What could we do? Our solution was to sit on the doorstep, as there were no chairs left in the house, and wonder or hope that our Mam would soon return. We tried knocking on the neighbour's doors, but they just ignored us and didn't bother coming out to see us or explain what had happened; they left us to our own devices. There we stayed, sat on the doorstep, for what seemed like forever, waiting and waiting for someone to come and look after us. We were cold, scared and on the verge of tears. This time there were no feelings of certainty in my stomach that we would be okay or about what was going to happen to us. It seemed like in a crisis it was more difficult for me to discern what may occur, as my thoughts were blinkered trying to deal with the current situation. My stomach was churning with fear.

The night was drawing in when eventually someone arrived to collect us. In actual fact, it was about two hours later when someone came; it was one of my Dad's friends. I recognized him from one or more boozy nights out he'd had with my Dad. Without any explanation he took us to another house, where to our delight we found our Mam and Dad. We thought we were never going to see them again, but they had actually moved to a new home without even thinking to tell us. We had never heard them discuss anything about a new house; for us the fact that we were moving, or indeed had actually moved, was a bolt from the blue. We soon settled down, though, after the surprise and massive shock we'd suffered, and all really liked our new home.

♦ ♦ ♦

MOVING IN WITH DAD

At the age of 14 I was allowed to move in with my Dad. I say allowed, but really there was no choice. It came about after one particular weekend, when there was a huge fight with Graham my stepdad. On the Saturday night of the weekend in question I was asleep with my brother Patrick in bed. We were both suddenly awoken by deafening shrieks and howling screams coming from downstairs; it sounded like someone was being murdered. We panicked. Although we were terrified by the absolute uproar we could hear, we had to find out what was going on. We sprinted downstairs as fast as we could.

Bursting into the kitchen, to our horror, we found Graham beating Mam with his fists. He was really laying into her. She was half-laid half-crouched on the floor, with her hands raised above her head, trying to protect herself from the pounding she was enduring. With no hesitation at all we both swung into action, and without saying a word to each other we grabbed Graham and threw him against the wall.

Working in unison we pinned him there, and with a few well aimed punches were able to stop him momentarily. At the time both Patrick and I were members of a boxing club, and luckily, we were both quite handy with our fists. But Graham was all riled up and wouldn't stop fighting and struggling, so eventually he had a right pasting. We knocked a few of his teeth out as well, but he managed to escape and ran out of the house shouting obscenities. His voice and threats faded down the road as he ran out of sight.

The door slammed. It was locked behind him. We thought and hoped that that was the last we'd be seeing of him for a while. We turned our attention to our poor mother who was in a right state. We tried to comfort her and tend to her bleeding nose and mouth, and her face which was beginning to bruise and swell like a balloon.

To our surprise, after only a short while, Graham was back hammering on the door snarling to be let back in, but everyone just ignored him, hoping he would go away. Then everything went silent. We waited with bated breath, wondering if something was about to happen. We all let out a sigh of relief when nothing did. However, within a matter of minutes of us thinking the worst was over, Graham was back again, and this time with a big woodman's axe.

He hacked away, trying to get through the door by chopping it down. Terrified, we stood and waited for the inevitable. We watched mesmerized as the door splintered and cracked. We could see the glint of the metal; the door was beginning to break under the strain of the blows and disintegrate in front of our eyes. It was exactly like the movie *The Shining*, where Jack Nicholson chops down the door. Suddenly the chopping and splintering stopped, and this was accompanied by the sound of sirens and shouting outside. We peered out of the window and saw that Graham had stopped in his tracks with the arrival of the police. Luckily for him, he'd heard them coming and had scarpered, but the police were in hot pursuit.

Even after what had happened, we knew Mam would take Graham back even though she had been really pulverized by him. I moved out of the family home pretty quick after that and moved in with my real Dad. True to form, Mam had taken Graham back and forgiven him before the bruises had been given a chance to heal. She didn't want me anywhere around spoiling things. There was also the fact that my stepdad wanted to give me a good thumping if he could get his hands on me, probably because of his lost teeth and pride. It was likely that he considered it was me who had knocked his teeth out and not Patrick; and he didn't seem bothered about getting any revenge on him.

With this in mind, I couldn't stay even if I wanted to. It's a bit of an understatement to say that I was definitely in his bad books. As a result, I moved in and lived with my real dad for the next ten years and these were the happiest days of my life. I have very fond memories of this period. Dad was my best friend and I can't express the words I felt when he died.

◆ ◆ ◆

THE PHONE STORY

My Dad's house was in a place called Thornaby in Stockton. One night, not long after moving in, and fast asleep in the spare room, I felt the bed being kicked. Jolting awake from my slumber, I thought it must have been one of those dreams that sometimes happens where you have a shock and jump awake. After a minute or two I dozed back off, but about three o'clock in the morning the phone downstairs rang. In my semi-conscious state, I dragged myself out from under the covers thinking I'd better answer the bleeding thing, but the other half of my mind was questioning how there was even a phone ringing, because we didn't have one that worked. All we had in the hallway was an old handset that was in the house when Dad moved in, and we had never got it fixed back up to re-join the network.

It was a big black old-fashioned phone with a dial that was covered in dust, and the wire had actually been cut so there was no possible way it could work. Getting downstairs to the handset I picked it up, wondering what the hell was going on, as being a bit more awake by then the reality that the phone wasn't even connected was sinking in. Still, my hand automatically picked up the receiver to answer. The moment I touched the phone it stopped ringing and the line was dead. There was nothing - not even a crackle, but I still checked to see if Dad had it reconnected without telling me. The line was just laid there, frayed on the floor. Totally mystified, I sat there for a while in the hallway with the severed line in my hands; I pondered the situation, trying to understand what had just happened and wondering if I was sane.

More and more of these little events began happening to me, at the time I just didn't understand what all of them meant. However, looking back I realise that it was my psychic side waking up and beginning to develop again. After my childhood experiences of somehow knowing things and seeing auras had all stopped, I had forgotten all about them. Now, I appreciate that these skills had become dormant for a while. Nonetheless they were slowly reawakening.

◆ ◆ ◆

LIVING WITH DAD

After moving back in with my real Dad, I decided to leave school as soon as possible and get a job to get a bit of money of my own to spend. Leaving school early at the age of 15, without bothering to do my exams, I went to work in Scotland as a steel erector. The earnings were incredible - about £200 per week - an extremely good wage for the time. But it wasn't permanent work - just short contracts. In those days it was a lot easier to find work, so I was able to get a lot of different jobs. After my work away finished, I always returned home to Dad's house.

During this period, I didn't bother with girls much they weren't a priority, but about age 24 I met a girl called Susie and adored her madly. She was my first true love, so I found myself falling head over heels for her. Inevitably we ended up moving in together, despite my father's better judgement. Dad warned me to keep away from her as he didn't think she was any good; his view was that she was a 'good time girl' since the minute my back was turned, she was always out enjoying herself. Dad was there while I was away working, and he watched her: on each and every occasion she was left by herself, my so-called girlfriend had other men round to stay. Me, being so blinded by my love for Susie, meant I didn't listen to the things Dad told me, and thought his judgment was clouded by his dislike for her.

The relationship didn't last long, though. One weekend on my early return to surprise Susie, wanting to see the look of delight on her face on my arrival home, I was about to be hit square in the face by my girlfriend's indiscretions. If only I had stayed in Scotland, blissfully unaware, but I was so excited and ran eagerly into the house. Susie wasn't downstairs, muffled sounds could be heard coming from upstairs. So, charging up as fast as possible and bursting into the bedroom, I was met with a sight that was a horror of horrors. There was Susie in bed with another man; they were both naked and all I could see was his little bare bum going up and down.

The real truth of what my girlfriend was actually like made me feel as if I'd been hit in the chest by a high-speed train. Devastated by Susie's betrayal, I realised my dad had been telling me the truth all along.

Without hesitating, I grabbed my stuff and marched out. Susie didn't bat an eyelid as she and this bloke continued enjoying each other's company. She had him moved in the same weekend. *Good luck to them* I thought, sarcastically, and had a feeling the new bloke would soon find himself in my shoes. So, however unexpectedly, there I was living back home with my Dad.

I often draw upon the anguish felt at the time of my split with Susie while helping other people through their own traumas during readings. Every experience in my life helps me empathise more with other people and their troubles.

♦ ♦ ♦

DAD'S ILLNESS

My father was not a well man; he'd had a bad chest for years. When he was eight years old, he caught pneumonia. He eventually recovered, but as soon as he felt well again, he began smoking, which was something the majority of people did in those days. From then on, he smoked for the rest of his life. He couldn't have stopped even if he'd wanted to, and he didn't. My father also suffered with a bad heart; his laboured breathing could be heard by me most nights when I was trying to get to sleep. It was quite unsettling and worrying.

On one night in particular when Dad was asleep, he could be heard gasping for breath. The air was rattling in his throat and was coming in very short puffs as he tried to breathe. I could hear him crying so went to check up on him, but he was crying in his sleep. There was only one thing I could think of doing to make sure he was okay, and that was to get into his bed with him to make sure he was alright. I stayed there looking after him all night. This night was particularly poignant, for it wasn't long after this that Dad died. I'd moved out again so blame myself for Dad's death; if I'd have still been living there taking care of him, he might not have become depressed and he would still be alive.

Dad's chest was so dreadful to endure that it dragged his mood down really low; he soon found himself inflicted with a bad case of depression. He was truly frightened of dying and he had been put on Valium by his doctor. The family decided we would try and make him feel better by taking him on holiday. We chose Greece as our destination, but Dad being depressed hadn't thought about his medication and didn't take enough with him. In hindsight we should have checked the amount he took along. Half way through the holiday Dad's tablets ran out and he went cold turkey. His withdrawal symptoms drove him mad; he felt he was going around the bend and was admitted to a Greek hospital.

When our family went to visit him, we found he'd disappeared. Obviously worried, we went out to search for him. After a bit of hunting around the neighbourhood I found myself drawn to a little street near the hospital where a wagon was parked. For some reason my feet, moving as if by themselves, walked me over to the wagon. It all seemed to happen in slow motion, and without knowing why I lifted the cover on the back of the wagon. I looked in.

The dreadful sight which met my eyes will never me; it will haunt me forever, because there in the back of the wagon was my dad hanging with his own belt. Dad was my world and I was absolutely devastated when he died, especially in such circumstances. Not surprisingly, Dad's death is still extremely emotional and difficult to talk about, even today. But as I relay these tragic events, there are small flashing lights appearing all around me.

◆ ◆ ◆

MAM'S ILLNESS

My Mam had been a diabetic for years, but her doctor hadn't realised so she wasn't put on the proper medication; eventually, she ended up in hospital. Mam had been put in a small ward with another three beds in the room. One night when I was visiting, I noticed a woman stood at the window. Normally this wouldn't catch my attention, but she turned looking directly at me and smiled. Straight away I thought: *that's my Grandmother.* I remembered her from being a child, but I didn't really know her well, as she'd died with me still a youngster. In surprise I turned to Mam and almost said to her 'look that's your Mam over there,' but didn't, as understandably I was a bit taken aback.

Later that day, my Mother was discharged from the hospital and went home. The staff obviously thought everything was going to be alright, but later that night she died peacefully in her sleep. It was only then the realisation dawned on me that my Grandmother had come to collect her daughter. This comprehension had eluded me as I was thinking that Gran had been there just for comfort and to keep an eye on Mam. Although sad, I've found comfort and reassurance in knowing that Mam didn't die alone, as Gran was there to assist and look after her.

◆ ◆ ◆

MY DEPRESSION

After Dad died, I reached a low point in my life, and started going to the pub every day to drown my sorrows. A good drink always made me feel better, but it was just a matter of time before the effects wore off and I started to need more than just alcohol to take away the feelings of pain and hopelessness.

With the shock of what had happened to Dad I felt I needed some help to get me back on track, so went to the doctors to see if they could be of assistance. Understandably the doctor thought I may be suffering with depression after the tragic experience with my father, but he didn't prescribe any medication. The Doctor thought it was a normal way to be, especially considering the circumstances surrounding Dad's death, and that I would start to feel better in time.

When people need help with depression during sittings it's easy now to explain, from personal experience, what depression feels like to me. I express it as being like a balloon that's being blown up, and eventually the outside of the balloon gets more and more tense until it pops.

My depression didn't lift with time but started building up over a number of years until eventually I did pop. I'd been working doing temporary jobs and was living quite comfortably in a flat, but I had no savings as I always immediately spent any money earned. However, with these constant feelings of anguish and upset I was in no fit state to continue working, and as a result ended up with no money to pay the rent. Therefore, in quite a short space of time, I found myself out on the streets sleeping rough.

Before long, I began sleeping on a bench in a churchyard; friends occasionally took me in where they could, so I was able to get a wash and sleep for a few nights on the settee before moving on.

After discovering what was happening to me my brother took me in; he had a spare room where I stayed, literally in bed, for about six months. During this time, I lost a great deal of weight and went down to about nine or ten stone, which is very underweight for my frame; normally I'm quite stocky.

Trying to pull myself together I visited the doctors again for help. This time they gave me some medication for depression, but they wanted to make more appointments to assess me for the despondent thoughts

I was having and the voices I was hearing. The voices were spirits trying to help me but being so depressed I tried to drown them out and was on a downward spiral.

Yet, instead of waiting for help from the doctor, for no reason I took off, and got a job helping to build a bridge in Halifax. It was while working on the bridge that I was starting to have erratic thoughts, mainly about how I should have done things differently to save my father.

Bad anxiety was also taking hold, which was getting worse and worse. Becoming very withdrawn, I felt like I was inside my body looking out at life but not taking part.

My life was being played out in front of me like a film, but it wasn't actually me participating in the movie. It felt more like I was watching someone else. When anyone tried to help me, I could still hear them talking to me, but didn't listen. I pushed anything they said to the back of my mind, not wanting to hear what they had to say.

Feeling completely knocked off my feet, it was at this point in my life that I needed someone to blame. I began focusing all my attention on my mother, making her the root cause of all my problems. My rationale was that if she hadn't been drinking every day and fooling around with other men, Mam and Dad would never have split up and we would have had a happy home life. I began to hate her, and daft thoughts kept coming into my head about things that had happened with Mam that made me hate her more.

They were silly little incidents, such as the time I remembered finding a pound and showed it to her all excited intending to spend it on sweets. She took it off me and said she would look after it and keep it safe, but that was the last I ever saw of my pound. In my mind everything bad that had happened in my life was her fault, no matter how small.

Thinking I was suffering with schizophrenia – not because of any voices as they had faded, but because there were so many bad thoughts that were alien to me running through my head – I eventually decided to see the doctor and told him about all the problems afflicting me. He told me it was not schizophrenia but a very bad case of depression; he gave me some more medication and sent me on my way, saying that was all that was wrong.

Soon after, the medication didn't seem to be working or hadn't kicked in. I was feeling desperate and felt like ending it all, so I went to North Tees Hospital and asked to be admitted, but they didn't want to take me in. They could see the state of me, and I told them I was going to commit suicide. The exact words used were 'I'm going to blow my brains out if you don't take me in because I can't stand it anymore.' Standing there, shaking in the hospital foyer, I was really frightened I was going to do something bad to myself. After many hours of waiting and pleading I was so relieved when they finally admitted me.

All these traumas that kept happening were awakening within me my psychic development. Each time something different happened, my psychic abilities enhanced a bit more and my skills developed at a faster rate. However, I was constantly trying to push them away and not allow them to surface. At that moment, my life was far too difficult to cope with without having these abilities to deal with as well.

Having been in North Tees Hospital for a while I was eventually put on the correct medication and was able to move in the right direction. Once I was released, I found it much easier to cope with my mental health issues, but today I still continue to suffer with bouts of depression and stay in bed for days as I can't seem to face the world.

People who know me say I am a man of extremes – either ecstatically happy and laughing, or in the pits of despair. I've recently been diagnosed with bi polar disorder as well, which seems to make sense. I find it easier to tackle my life day by day rather than thinking of the future.

◆ ◆ ◆

LIVING IN MY BROTHER'S FLAT

Still suffering with depression and on medication, I lived in a flat above an electrical shop belonging to my eldest brother John. I was reasonably content, had lived there for a while quite happily, and felt my life was getting back on track. However, this all changed one night when there was an enormous thumping on the door.

This thumping sounded like someone was trying to break in with a sledge-hammer. I was fast asleep in bed at the time of this thudding, so I jumped awake, startled and completely disorientated. I couldn't quite work out what the noise was or where it had come from. Before I had time to worry about this though, the crashing started again.

I jumped out of bed, burst outside my room and ran along the passage leading to the front door. The silence perplexed me when I got to the door. So, there I stood, waiting with bated breath to see if whoever it was would bang again. There was no more pounding. I gingerly opened the door after a few minutes but there was no one about. Puzzled, I went back to bed. I simply thought that some drunk must have come to the wrong house, or that there was some other similar explanation.

The next night, as the hours of darkness descended, I managed to fall into a disturbed sleep. Again, I was jolted awake by a tremendous hammering on the front door. This sudden noise left me wondering what or who the hell it could be and why they were harassing me. I paid attention to the sounds and thought about what might be happening. I considered it could have been a drug dealer turning up to the wrong house.

The thumping stopped, but footsteps of what sounded like a large, heavy man could be heard walking up the passage, echoing the heavy blows. This was totally unexpected; *how did they manage to get in?* I thought. Gripped with fear I clung to the covers. I listened; the footsteps stopped right outside my bedroom, but the pounding at the front door began again. Feeling petrified; my stomach churned, and I was unsure what to do next. The only thing I could think of doing was to creep out of bed and listen.

Not brave enough to step into the passageway, I hid safely behind the bedroom door. It was obvious this wasn't a good plan though, as the door was made of thin flimsy panels which would offer no protection whatsoever - especially, as the footsteps suggested, from a burly man. Once again, the pounding started, and it was followed by the same laborious heavy thud climbing the passage. Yet again, they halted at my bedroom door and then the silence resumed.

◆ ◆ ◆

After about ten minutes of waiting, I shivered, wide-eyed, behind the door. It took me all my strength to summon the nerve to open it. Quiet and tentative, I grasped the handle. Little by little, I pulled the door, so it showed a crack I was able to peep through. With the door slightly ajar, I surveyed the passage in secret. Incredulously, no-one was there. Nor was there a sign of anything untoward. I walked to the front door; the bolt was still on and there was no sign of forced entry. I was completely baffled and confused by this pattern of chilling events.

In dismay I slumped on the passage floor in the doorway, wondering what was happening to me. I thought I was going mad; I dreaded to imagine what others might think of me if I told them about the activities being experienced in my flat. It was easier to blame it on my medication, and I didn't tell anyone for fear they would think I was going barmy. Thankfully, nothing happened for a few nights. I was just starting to relax, thinking the events must have been nightmares or my imagination. It was too soon to take things easy, though, as that night the pounding returned louder than ever.

◆ ◆ ◆

I leapt out of bed. Before I'd had the chance to shake myself awake properly, I ran to the front door, half asleep. Fear made me stop short of opening it. The hairs on the back of my neck stood up; I'd suddenly gone really cold and beads of sweat trickled down my forehead. In that hushed moment, everything silenced. I could see my breath, but my memory of the footsteps came flooding back.

In my sudden recollection I decided to edge around in an attempt to lean against the door. I stood completely still, and with trepidation stared intently into the gloomy passage.

I thought whoever had caused the thudding would materialise. I panted in short rasps and my steaming, white breath filled the air. I waited, anxious, but a wave of tiredness struck me when I began to calm down. At this precise second, the pounding started again.

Still slouched; my back was leaning on the door. I almost jumped out of my skin with the enormous hammering noise behind me. It vibrated through my entire body. It gave me such a shock that it made me tumble to the floor, yet, at the same time, my feet were glued to the spot and I couldn't move or envisage who might be out there at this hour.

An impulse took over me and shook me from my panic-stricken state. I found courage from deep within and yelled expletives through the letter box, at the top of my voice. My rationale was that if the shouting was loud enough it would scare off whatever or whoever was out there.

Instantly, the pounding stopped. There was a deathly silence. I waited, holding my breath. After some time, everything seemed to have settled down. I returned to bed, but, unsurprisingly, it took me quite a while to calm down. My adrenaline was pumping still; my body was shaking, and I lay quaking under the covers. Somehow, though, I was enveloped by a feeling of deep confidence that the pounding would never happen again, I didn't know why, but I understood profusely that this particular experience was over.

♦ ♦ ♦

The nights were now quiet, so my confidence the banging torment had ended was justified. A new strange activity was happening, though: I was now seeing things. The living room door was half-glass and half-wood. One night, while I was watching television, I was chilled by a sight that met the corner of my eye: someone walked past on the other side of the glass. There was definitely no one else in the flat - I was without doubt by myself; there was no one else living with me and the flats both sides were empty. There was also the big bolt on the front door which was locked. It was the only way in or out, so no one had broken in. I told myself it must be hallucinations and it couldn't be real, so I tried to not take much notice.

As the weeks went by these occurrences increased, and I started smelling things as well. It was just whiffs at first, but then there were smells that seemed to linger. It was like I knew what these were but couldn't quite place them. These goings-on made me feel uneasy, like there was something in the flat with me.

One unforgettable night, when I was on the brink of sleep, I heard the pained groaning of a man. It was inches away from me, and this groan sounded like this man's last breath. My eyes shot open; my heartbeat accelerated. A feeling of dread which made me go cold accompanied the moan. I was frozen to the core, and colder than I'd ever been. A tremendous fear gripped me.

Imagine, the sound of someone giving their last breath in your ear as you lay in bed. Yet, no-one else is there, and you are unable to see the source of the sound. The experience was terrifying; I was petrified and paralysed with fear, but there were no more noises or groans.

I tried to rationalise the situation, because otherwise I'd never be able to sleep again. I stared at the pillow next to me. There was obviously no-one there, so I put the noise down to anything I could think of, like tyres screeching or people messing about outside. Just about every unlikely scenario I could think of hurtled through my mind.

Somehow, I pushed the moan which had just rattled me to the back of my thoughts. I'd finally persuaded myself that it was a noise from outside and settled into sleep.

♦ ♦ ♦

The next day my brother asked me to do him a favour, which was to help shift some bulky items he couldn't manage himself. Loading his van, I began to explain the episodes in the flat. I suggested the building might be haunted. My brother called me a daft bastard and thought it was all rubbish, but I insisted that the flat had spooks roaming around terrorising me. John wasn't taking me seriously even though I must have looked dreadful from lack of sleep and had big dark bags under my eyes. Therefore, I decided to take matters into my own hands. I visited the parish priest to see if he could do anything to help, as this phenomenon was actually getting very scary.

The priest said he would sort the problem out, and the next day came with his holy water and incense to bless the flat. He went from room to room giving blessings and shaking holy water over the surroundings; he told me there would be no more problems.

Over the next few weeks there were no more incidents, so the blessing had apparently worked. I began to relax again. Thankfully, things were back to the normal run of the mill.

◆ ◆ ◆

I felt it was now possible to relax again in my own home, so I began to chill out. This was short lived, however, until a couple of nights later. I was alone as usual, dressed only in my underpants, and was making a cup of tea in the kitchen.

Totally out of the blue, an anguished groan reverberated right behind me. A shiver ran down my spine. Covered in goosebumps, I spilled water all over the worktop; luckily, I didn't scald myself.

I turned around, slowly, expecting to see someone behind me, but no-one was there. Each hair on my body raised like the hackles of a cat, and my pulse thudded in my ears. My heart felt like it was thrashing about in my throat.

I walked backwards towards my bedroom. It sounded like the groan was directly in front of me, but there was nothing there. For a moment I thought I could smell rancid hot breath on my face. I panicked, knowing I had to get out of the flat. Full pelt action ensued.

If someone had been watching it must have been comical, as I was running around like a headless chicken. I attempted to pull on my trousers, put on my shoes and find my keys all at the same time. My goal was to vacate the flat as quickly as possible. Absolutely terrified and in so much of a fluster, I tripped and crashed into the front door. I banged my head, but at the same time pulled frantically at the bolt.

Following much jiggling and heaving the bolt gave way. I flung open the door and was out of the flat in a jolt; I was hugely relieved to have escaped into the cold fresh air. The outside had never felt as good. I stood there, half-dressed in the dark, shaking like a leaf. I swallowed large gulps of air, trying to still my rapid breathing and end the hammering in my chest.

Behind me the door swung shut with a loud bang. This made me jump and I began to run, wondering where to go in my half-dressed state. My brother Patrick had a house nearby where I immediately headed. He wasn't very happy that I'd woken him in the early hours, but I must have looked a right state. I stood there with a cut forehead and bruised eye, dishevelled and quivering.

So far, this was the most horrifying thing that I'd encountered. It was even scarier than the thumping of the sledge hammer on my door and to this day it's still one of the most terrifying experiences.

◆ ◆ ◆

Eventually Patrick took pity on me. He let me stay, and I stopped there for a couple of nights. My other brother John, who came to visit during this time, took my gibbering about the flat seriously when he saw the clip of me. He told his friends and discovered one of them knew a medium. Through his friend Maggie, John managed to get in touch with this medium called Tony who was quite famous locally.

Tony visited the flat, but I didn't go with him as I was far too petrified. Tony told me afterwards that there was the spirit of an old gentleman present in the flat; he had been the owner of the shop below. He was a butcher and the shop used to be a butcher's shop. The man had actually died outside of the bedroom on the landing which happened to be the room where I slept.

Over the years the spirit of the butcher man had frightened all of the other residents out of the premises. By all accounts, he hadn't been a very nice man when he was alive, and he was continuing the trait now he was dead. I told Tony about getting the local priest to bless the house, and he explained that if you are not a religious man when you're alive, you are not a religious man when you're dead. Apparently - with the stories only now being told by neighbours after they'd heard about my experience - this butcher man had not been religious in any way shape or form and had no fear of God. According to Tony, when the priest blessed the house and said the prayers, they had no effect on his spirit, because with him not believing in God and having no fear of him when he was alive, he had no fear when he was dead. So, he was still here staying in our plane of existence. Tony sent the spirit on his way, whatever that meant, and explained that it would be okay to return to the flat as there wouldn't be any more problems. So, with much apprehension I moved back in. True to the Medium's word the flat was fine - in fact the atmosphere now felt quite pleasant.

Before leaving, Tony said he had some information that he needed to pass onto me; he began explaining a few things about my Dad. These were personal things that I was very grateful to hear. I want to keep them personal, so I won't go into them, but he didn't stop there. He went on to tell me that I had mediumship skills like him; I had no idea what he was on about and told him so. Tony wasn't perturbed and continued impressing on me that I had a gift, and that my Dad was there telling him I was going to be a Medium.

Tony didn't listen to my remonstrating but continued on with even more unbelievable information. He tried telling me that I had a Red Indian chap stood next to me and that he was going to be my spirit guide. Imagine this scenario: I'd had nothing to do with spiritualism, and even though Tony had seemingly got rid of the spirit haunting my flat, I still couldn't get my head round all these 'woo-woo' ideas. Being very sceptical, I wanted to know the name of this Red Indian fellow; Tony told me the Red Indian would enlighten me when he was ready, and not before.

To say I considered this was all a load of nonsense was an understatement. However, it transpired that the haunting in my flat had stopped. After I returned and settled back down in to everyday life, the things Tony had told me sparked my curiosity - so much so that I decided to begin going to the spiritualist church. There, I would endeavour to learn more about myself and my Indian spirit guide.

♦ ♦ ♦

Carrie Roberts

MY FIRST EXPERIENCES OF THE SPIRITUALIST CHURCH

After completing some research, it was easy to discover a spiritualist church not too far from me; although I was quite apprehensive not knowing what to expect, I decided to attend. The place was simple to find, but on my arrival, I felt a bit anxious as, not understanding much about spiritualism, I worried it might be like a cult or some similar practice. I hung about outside for a while watching the regulars go in and tried to pluck up the courage to walk inside. Eventually curiosity overcame me, and I crept quietly through the doors, discreetly, trying not to be noticed.

Inside everyone looked normal. They were all sat down in pews chatting to each other like regular people. This began to make me feel better; I wasn't as different from everyone else as I thought I would be. The people weren't dressed in pointy hats or capes - in fact, amazingly, I started to feel excited, albeit still a little anxious. I looked around and studied the faces of the people in the room; to me they seemed eager, each having an expectant glint to their eyes. Quietly, I slipped into a seat at the back of the church and waited.

A few minutes later a man came out and stood on a platform at the front of the church. He was a little, aged man with a ruddy face; he glanced at everybody in the room and began talking. He was talking about treating everybody you meet as you would like to be treated; I wasn't really listening to what he had to say, as I took more interest in watching his audience to gauge their reactions.

This old man stayed there, expounding for a while; he had bottle-top specs and, unnervingly, seemed intrigued by me as he kept looking in my direction. My anxiety began to resurface and get the better of me. I didn't like the way he was staring, so I put my head down and tried to hide and slipped further into the pew. I was absolutely crapping myself, but I didn't have the courage to get up and leave. This was the very first time I'd ventured into a spiritualist church; I was there alone, feeling extremely uncomfortable, and wondering if the congregation would all begin chanting or turn on me.

I soon realised there was no need to worry. No one else seemed to notice me, and eventually the speaker said he was going to give people messages from the spirit world. *Good, I thought now it was starting to get more interesting.* I wasn't expecting it, but he immediately looked to the back of the church and directly at me. The next words he said were about wanting to speak with that young man in the red top.

My mouth went dry; I looked down at my bright red top, wanting to disappear. I hoped the floor would open up and swallow me. Contemplating what the old man wanted, I sat there, meekly, watching him, but was totally amazed with the next thing he said. Out of nowhere, he began talking about a Red Indian chap who was stood next me.

Thoughts began racing through my mind about the other bloke Tony, the Medium, who also told me that. Incredibly they'd both come up with the same thing. *They can't both know about me*, I thought. As I knew they hadn't had the opportunity to talk to each other about me, I started to pay attention to what the speaker had to say. Plucking up the courage, I heard myself asking, in a rather timid voice, what the Red Indian's name was. Again, I was given the same reply as provided by Tony: that when the time was right, I would find out. He also said he could see me stood up there on the rostrum - which is the platform at the front of the church where the speaker stands - doing the same thing he was doing:

giving messages to people. My immediate thought was that I wouldn't be doing any of that carry on, but that was twice now I'd been given the exact same bizarre information.

◆ ◆ ◆

FIRST PROPER MESSAGE

The things both mediums had said kept repeating in my head, and I began to wonder what it would be like to receive messages for people. Constantly mulling these things over must have made me more open to hearing spirit, because I did start to get thoughts in my head that weren't mine. It wasn't like when I was depressed and ill, getting alien thoughts about wanting to die to put a stop to the misery. These new thoughts were sort of mundane, and they came to me when I was around other people.

The first time I decided to act on one of these thoughts was just a normal day, much like any other. I was stuck in, waiting for the TV repairman to come to fix the aerial. In the meantime, I sat around quite bored, twiddling my thumbs and uninterested in what was on the radio or in the paper. Eventually, the man arrived and got his ladders out to fix the TV. He told me his name was Jack; he was by himself, so, feeling kind hearted, I offered to lend a hand. Jack was very grateful and asked if it would be alright if I could hold the ladders for him.

We chatted for a few minutes. Jack was at the top of the ladders, and I holding onto the bottom, when suddenly strange thoughts about people unknown to me flooded my mind. These were thoughts and images about two women who were out shopping. While wondering what was going on, yet sort of knowing why these odd thoughts were racing through my head, I struggled for a few minutes trying to comprehend how to proceed. An urge came over me to shout up the ladder, so I decided resolutely that's what I would do and asked in a rather loud voice if Jack knew anyone called Jane. He replied that Jane was his wife, so I continued, and enquired if he knew someone called Marie. Again, Jack knew this person and she turned out to be his daughter. Laughingly, I said it was my duty to inform him to be careful because they were out on a shopping spree spending all his hard-earned cash.

Jack stepped slowly down the ladder looking bewildered and wanting to know exactly what was going on. He asked if his wife and daughter had put me up to this, and, if so, the reason why. It could have turned nasty in other circumstance, but luckily Jack was an amiable sort of bloke. I explained my path as a budding medium, and if a message came to me it had to be passed on; these messages were being received for him for some reason.

This was not only the first time I'd ever passed on a message this way, but also the first time I'd plucked up the courage to speak about the things I could hear and see. It was quite exciting, as I'd voiced the things being received. Talking to a complete stranger like this was an absolute novelty; never before had I been able to overcome the hurdle of speaking to an unfamiliar person about the awareness, thoughts and understanding of someone else's life. I was overawed and curious about how this knowledge wound up in my head, and also very pleased the details given were so correct, even down to the accurate names. It had only been a short message, but it was merely the start of a long line of messages which I began to receive. From now on I'd certainly begin paying attention to this 'gift', because it should be considered remarkable.

♦ ♦ ♦

MESSAGES TODAY

Often today, if I receive a message from the spirit world, it will usually be when I'm in mid-conversation with someone. This makes me stop and look to the side of the person I'm speaking with to say 'hello' to the spirit. After greeting the spirit in this manner, I'll just carry on talking; it has become commonplace for me to do this without thinking. The person chatting will look to see who I'm speaking to, but when they realise it's a spirit making contact they quite often freak out; this especially happens if they haven't met or spoken to me before. The spirit may not be there for the particular person in front of me, but for someone else who will be meeting me in the next few days. This type of thing is second nature to me as it happens all the time, but for other people it's quite mystifying.

Every so often, when I'm booked to do a reading, a spirit will appear a few days before and follow me around. They don't normally speak as they're just waiting to get in touch with their loved ones and are eager to give their message. For instance, I could be sat eating my tea and someone will walk into the room and sit waiting in silence; it could be that I'm walking around the local supermarket and a spirit will pop out from one of the aisles, follow me home and stay for the rest of the day. They tend to do this as they want to make sure they can make contact with me, so they will definitely get through to their loved one when the moment comes. This is understandable; it's simply that the spirits get excited and can't wait until the reading. We all get excited about things and can't wait for them to happen. Apparently, even spirit still get this feeling - it's a bit like when people queue early for the sales.

When giving a reading, I can pick up messages in different ways. From time to time there's a flash of light, together with a picture that appears in my mind. This image is of how the person looked when they were alive combined with an accompanying feeling attached with it. Other times it's possible to actually see them physically. To explain this further, for instance, with a feeling of a large man there is a sensation of me growing bigger; if the spirit is smaller like an old woman, the sensation is me shrinking down. This enables me to feel the physical characteristics that the person had when they were in this life, and then I convey them on to the people at the reading to see if they comprehend them.

On occasion the full package arrives: that is, the sense of the size, shape, health and ability of the person when they were alive, the feelings that they had from their lifetime such as love, regret etc. An image of what they look and sound like, and what they are trying to convey, all fill my mind and body. This is an intense experience which enables me to pass on a much more detailed understanding or interpretation. On occasion transfiguration can occur: this is where the face of the spirit making contact appears over my face for the person receiving the reading to see.

This happened once for a man who was receiving messages from his Dad; towards the end of the reading I felt very close to this spirit and so asked the son if he wanted to actually see his Dad. The man looked at me, dumbfounded, but as his father's face began to take shape over mine the man's face lit up. He got really excited, shouting, "I can see him, I can see him. I can see me Dad!" This only happens for a moment, and then I return back to normal.

Well this man was ecstatic; he jumped up and ran around the room saying, "I saw me Dad" repeatedly. Then, he ran up to me, placed a big smacker on the side of my face, and gave me a big hug. After this he ran into the other room to tell everyone else what had just happened. When I left, he was still on cloud nine; he looked like he was going to jump up and click his heels together, he was on that much of a high. It is difficult to express how these things happen; these messages are received in whatever form and must be passed on to the appropriate people. If this doesn't happen, I'm tormented by the thoughts and feelings rushing through my head, but it's good and really satisfying for me when readings are received in such a happy manner.

To speak to the other side, my channels of communication are 'open.' Everyone has seven energy centres or chakras, to use the correct terminology, and a way to keep them open is to imagine each one as a door. For me the doors are open all the time; if they are closed then communication is closed down. It's reassuring for me to keep them open constantly, because there's a fear that if I 'close down' by shutting the doors, my gift might not come back.

This happened to me once and it was very traumatic, except unbeknown to me I was being given a rest. At the time I found myself totally grounded for a couple of weeks, not being able to feel, hear, see or sense anything from the other side, and didn't know what to do with myself. It was so strange as I'd grown accustomed to spirits always being around, and it was a weird couple of weeks when they weren't there anymore. Later, when my gift came back, it was stronger. So, it was then I realised I'd been closed down for a reason, as my body and mind were being tuned to a higher vibration. This enabled me to do a better job; I was able to be more specific and precise in the evidence I passed on to people.

Nonetheless, having said that, I wish at least once a week that this gift wasn't mine; sometimes it weighs heavily on my shoulders and feels like a huge responsibility. This is especially so when you have someone sat in front of you who is very vulnerable, or someone who wants spiritual guidance. The spirit's message must be passed on exactly with the correct understanding, and not my interpretation. Occasionally, this can be difficult. For example, a person may get a message to take more care of themselves because they have been getting pains in the chest. Now, if you don't expand on that message to, for example, say the pains in the chest are from indigestion, the person may go home thinking they're going to have a heart attack if they don't make a drastic change. So, you must make sure you pass on the right message, and, equally, that the person listening has understood the message correctly. With this approach you can put their mind at rest, and they can go away happy. It's probably like being a counsellor in a way, as you must have unconditional positive regard and not be tempted to colour messages with your own experiences or advice.

◆ ◆ ◆

CONSULTATION WITH THE DOCTOR

Shortly after the events in the flat it was time to return to North Tees Hospital, where my depression had been diagnosed; I needed to make sure I was getting on okay with my medication and mental state. My name was called to see the doctor, and upon walking into the consultation room noticed a book on the paranormal on a table. The doctor started with the niceties of telling me to take a seat, and asking how I was feeling, etc. However, I didn't pay much attention to what he was saying because there was the spirit of a man standing behind him. Focusing on what the doctor said while this man was stood looking at me was an impossible task; so, nodding to the book, I asked if the doctor believed in all that paranormal stuff.

As the opportunity had arisen, I jumped in with both feet before he had the chance to answer. I explained I don't really know much about it either, but that my profession is actually talking to dead people. A look appeared on the doctor's face as if to say: *yes, we've got a bit of a 'looney tune' here - we'll have him strapped up with his arms behind his back in no time.* Persevering, thinking *what have I got to lose*, I began explaining there was a gentleman stood behind him. The doctor, not surprisingly, looked at me blankly. He said "Pardon?" in a confused manner, while trying to look to the rear over his shoulder. Persisting, I told him again that there was a man stood behind him and said: *"I think he's your father."*

At the same time a conversation with the spirit was taking place in my head. He was firmly impressing on me: "I don't *think* I'm his father, *I am* his father." I decided to speak out loud, so the doctor could hear what was going on; I persisted by asking the spirit to tell me his name and I heard 'Robert' in my head. The answer was put quite plainly so the doctor would understand: "The gentleman says he is your father and his name is Robert."

The doctor looked incredulous; he was blinking furiously and had turned the same shade of white as his coat. He was trying to take all this in, so it was easy just to keep talking. I continued by explaining the things he had been doing over the last few days, and that he was contemplating going on a fishing holiday if he could fit it in to his busy schedule, I also told him a few more personal things.

By the time we'd finished, the doctor was now a funny shade of grey; he sat quietly for a few moments, assimilating the information he'd been given. The doctor's world must have been turned upside down: there he was, a man of science having the world of spirit shoved in his face without warning. To my surprise, it looked like he was beginning to accept it. This was unbelievable, especially when he concluded that, in his opinion, I didn't have any mental health problems at all, but had a 'gift'. This astounded me and echoed in my mind because that's also what the medium Tony had told me.

The conversation continued, as the thing was, I still had depression, but it had been much better with me on the medication. Even though he decided mental health problems weren't an issue, I was still prescribed the medication to help with my mood. Sadly, I never saw that particular doctor again and often wonder if he became a believer in the afterlife and mediums, or if he just said he didn't want to see me again, and so had me removed from his list of patients.

◆ ◆ ◆

THE STORY OF MY SPIRIT GUIDES NAME

The Red Indian man, whom two mediums had described to me, kept popping into my head; I became more and more curious about him. It seemed very strange to me that an invisible Red Indian was following me around, and consequently, I was interested to know if it was true that such a guide existed. Not knowing this Indian's name was also beginning to annoy me; so, on a night, I would lie in bed and ask in my mind what the name of the Red Indian was. I tried to remember all the names I could think of that I'd seen in the movies, such as *Running Water, Sitting Bull, Runs like the Wind*. I asked if any of these were the right name, but nothing stuck in my mind as a reply, and no answer came to me.

After a couple of months of persevering with this, I began to think I would never get a response. One night at about 2am, I was unable to sleep, so I questioned my spirit guide striving to find his name. I decided to change my method and posed questions in my thoughts instead of just reciting a list of names.

When still nothing was forthcoming, I got annoyed, lost my temper, and shouted in my head: *'Come on then; tell me your name.'* Again, nothing happened; there was no imminent answer. Except this time, after a few moments, a presence seemed to connect with me. This made me feel that my Red Indian friend was there paying attention to the questions I posed.

It wasn't the fact that I could see something or someone, but more of an awareness of a presence which wasn't previously discernible in the room with me. Without warning, a voice boomed in my mind, saying quite loudly and clearly: *'Hawks Wing.'* I assumed at first that this must be me imagining things, but slowly it dawned on me the voice I could hear was someone else's voice.

Not believing what had just taken place and thinking it was a trick of my imagination, I began the ritual of repeating names again: *'Tell me if your name is Flies like an Eagle or Runs Like a Wolf,'* and again, in a clear, deep voice, in a sort of pidgin English accent: *'No, Hawks Wing'* bellowed once again.

◆ ◆ ◆

The next day, still not convinced about what I'd heard, I went to bed. Following the same routine as each previous night, I asked the question: *'Tell me if your name is Sitting Bull,'* etc. On every occasion I would hear the reply *'Hawks Wing'* but each time the response loudened. I continued this practice habitually for about a month, but I still thought the answer was my imagination. Each time the answer grew louder still. The real problem was, that I couldn't get my head round the idea that a Red Indian man was following me about and talking to me.

I must mention here that in the meantime I had met and fallen in love with a woman. We had a daughter together; we had since split up and didn't live together, but I still helped to look after my child.

This state of affairs with my spirit guide was still continuing, when one day I went to pick my daughter up from school. It was such a bright, sunny day that we decided to walk home over the field. As we walked along, chatting, we saw what looked like a little bundle of feathers. Being curious, we sauntered over to see what it was.

As we got closer, we looked more intently at the feathers; soon, I held the little bundle securely in my hands. In holding it up it was clear to see that the bundle was the single wing of a bird, but not just any bird: it was that of a kestrel or a hawk! In that moment of instant realisation that it was a hawk's wing, I felt a massive rush through my body, and simultaneously, a loud voice thundered in my mind: *'I told you what my name was, and **that** is my name, **HAWKS WING**.'*

It was the loudest spirit voice I had ever heard. Even today there has been nothing else like it. It gave me such a jolt I nearly fell over. I was overwhelmed with shock. I quickly slung down the feathers, while at the same time, I could feel the colour draining from my face; every single hair on my body was standing on end. I grabbed my daughter's hand, and we ran home as fast as we could. She was blissfully unaware of my astonishment and was trying to pick daisies and buttercups as we ran along. When we eventually got home, I looked in the mirror and was as white as a sheet. I needed a few minutes to calm down and digest what had just happened.

Since then, needless to say, there has never been any need to question my guide's name. I now realise the relentless monotony of my questioning must have been getting really exasperating. Hawks Wing is here to help and guide me in my communications with the spirit world, and I have also had the piece of good fortune to see Hawks Wing physically.

He was stood there, right in front of me one day, in full tribal regalia with a long-feathered head dress; I felt very privileged. Another time, when looking in the mirror, I saw Hawks Wing's face peering back at me; he had full face paint which gave me a surprise at first, but it was such an honour to be shown his true appearance.

From my communications with Hawks Wing I have learned that the Red Indians are a race of people whom are very private individuals. At first, Hawks Wing didn't like me to tell the story of how his name was discovered, but now he has got used to it being told. So, it's nice that we are both learning together as we go along.

◆ ◆ ◆

SPIRIT GUIDES

Over the years many different spirit guides have been and gone; but, since becoming aware of Hawks Wing, he has been with me permanently. Every now and then, different guides will appear for a short period of time to help with a current situation or problem. There are also other guides who are always present.

One of those constantly nearby is a Roman man called Anthony, who just seems to be on the edge of things, watching over me for protection. Another guide, who hangs around in the background, is a big Afro-Caribbean man called Emtembi; he never speaks and is with me to safeguard me from evil.

There are lots of other guides too, such as Sister Mary Catherine who is a healer and was a Catholic Nun in her lifetime. She comes when I do spiritual healing. Then, many other guides pop in and out from time to time when they are needed.

Everyone has guides, whether they are aware of them or not. When giving a reading for someone, it is initially the person's guide who comes through and tells me all the things the individual has been doing lately. People find this amazing, but this is proof for the person that I am really receiving information that is correct and genuine.

After communicating with the guide, it's the turn of family members or friends who have passed over to come through; it allows them to give a message or to just say hello. This helps whoever is receiving the reading to know that the people who have passed are alright: that they are still around and interested in what's going on in the lives of their family and friends.

◆ ◆ ◆

THE START OF GIVING MESSAGES

Many people had started asking me for readings, news of my growing spiritual skills had travelled fast through my friends and acquaintances. As a result, there were a lot of readings to be undertaken which were charged at five pounds per person. Many people were interested in contacting friends or relatives on the other side who thought five pounds was quite cheap; for that reason, most of my evenings were taken up with my new-found fame. Hitherto, I hadn't really learnt to develop or control my gift properly and was always 'switched on'. This meant my channels of communication with the spirit world always remained open. Therefore, my availability was 24/7 access to any spirit who wanted to contact me any time, day or night.

As a result, it didn't matter where I might be. Spirits were constantly about; whether at the shop or in the swimming pool, there would always be a spirit trying to talk to me. This was becoming very draining on my energy, as I hadn't yet been taught that there was a way to switch off. As luck would have it, in the pub one night, I recognised a man called Jim who was from the spiritualist church. We began talking, and as he was into spirit stuff it was easy to explain to him about seeing spirits everywhere. Jim said he thought it was about time I went up on the rostrum to give some messages. He further explained that it was time to attend a circle, where I could learn to develop my gift. So, with Jim's help, I began to attend, and after a while I arranged my first service.

To explain, a development circle can be a monthly gathering that is open to anyone who wants to learn more about or explore and grow their connections to the spirit world. It is usually an ongoing group, often held at a spiritualist church, in which techniques for enhancing mediumship talents are practiced. Discussions are also held to address concerns, issues and struggles that people may be experiencing and these are very helpful. Being a member of a development circle is a great way to increase ability and skill. A circle will normally contain a group of people who want to improve their budding psychic abilities, such as: clairvoyance, psychometry, mediumship, energy healing, and other similar methods.

There are many benefits of participating in a circle, and the format allows like-minded individuals to come together. This helps them share a sense of unity when advancing their potential. When I attended, I felt it was reassuring to meet other people with a similar interest. Participants may also learn more about themselves, which can lead to a greater sense of personal happiness, as well as compassion towards others. The development circle also allows each individual to grow in a way that suits their level of understanding. It provides balance, as people who are at varying stages of growth are able to help each other to progress.

As with most things, some people benefit more than others from widening their knowledge. Although my attending the development circle was an insightful way to find out more about what was happening to me in the long term, I felt this activity wasn't for me. However, I did attend a fair few sessions and found them very useful, especially when they taught me how to 'close down' my abilities when I needed to. They explained remaining 'open' all the time can be quite draining for a person, leaving them very tired. Thanks to these teachings, I was now aware it was a choice and that I could 'close down' if I needed to.

♦ ♦ ♦

MY FIRST PROPER CHURCH SERVICE

Sat on the rostrum at the front of the spiritualist church; the day I was anticipating with both fear and dread, but also a bit of excitement, was finally here. After attending meetings with the development circle for a few months, I'd found myself talked into speaking at a service. Hence, there I sat, in front of everyone in the church, in full view of the congregation, who were staring at me expectantly. I thought to myself *'this is proper weird' and* doubted my ability. I wondered what on earth I was doing there; my mind was going into overdrive. Deciding the people in charge had made a mistake - that I had no business being up there and should in actual fact be in the audience - I began looking for an escape. But as far as I could see there was no way out.

The longer I sat there the more I worried. I was nervous, and there was absolutely nothing coming to me - no messages, nothing – so, I was starting to agonize that my debut was going to be the biggest flop ever. Then the speaker's voice boomed, announcing my formal name: James MacCann. He introduced me as a newcomer, and it soon dawned on me that my agony was finally here. The speaker explained that I was going to get up, show my clairvoyance skills, and hopefully give some messages. *No such luck,* I thought, but managed to stand even though my legs were weak. I wondered if the audience could sense my fear or see the beads of sweat breaking out on my face. Thoughts raced through my head as I contemplated my fate. I thought there was no way I could manage to do what was expected of me and felt as if my legs were about to buckle. Realistically I was more likely to throw up than tell people anything useful.

Nonetheless, as soon as I stepped forward a phenomenal change took hold; a feeling of certainty enveloped me, and by some amazing, wonderful miracle, I promptly started talking. I sensed the very first message was for a lady, who was wearing a black cardigan, and sat near the front of the audience. I asked if she understood the name Elizabeth. She explained she had an auntie by that name, but before she could finish more words tumbled from my mouth and it carried on from there. Even though there was still a patch of sweat in the middle of my back, and I could feel it running down my spine, I began to feel right at home. I could see spirits lined up, waiting their turn to speak to me. By the end of the meeting I was shaking with exhilaration. I'd noticed that as the service went on, it felt better and easier to me as I delivered more messages. All the communications seemed to be right, and as a result I gained more confidence.

At the conclusion of the service I was naturally very relieved; it was all over, but I was ecstatic. Although I couldn't exactly say the entire event had been enjoyable from start to finish, it had been an incredible experience which I wanted to repeat as soon as possible.

However, I discovered after a few turns on the rostrum that the church wasn't really for me; it felt like I didn't really fit in. The problem being I would get over-excited and tended to swear quite a lot as a result; this is not the done thing in church, so I concentrated more on doing private readings. Later on, though, I moved back into giving church services when I had gained more experience. I wasn't quite so excitable at this stage; therefore, could manage to keep my language under control and deliver readings with more composure.

◆ ◆ ◆

THE PSYCHIC FAIRS

My reputation was still spreading, and a lot of people were asking for readings from me. I started doing heaps of private sittings for people – strangers as well as friends. This helped me to gain more experience and skill as I was still a bit unsure of myself in the outset.

One day, someone showed me an ad in the local paper. It was for an afternoon of 'clairvoyance'. So, incredibly interested and curious, I went along. The fair was being held at a hall in Stockton, and upon entering I saw three ladies sat behind tables with their names in large print in front of them. The services they offered were also on display, such as: 'tarot readings' or 'medium'. There were a few people waiting, so I decided to hang around while trying to listen to conversation. I was inquisitive to see how other people operate, and maybe even get myself a reading.

There was a lady called Pauline advertising herself as a Medium. She had a small queue of people that she seemed to work through pretty quickly; when it was my turn, she beckoned me over, calling me 'love' and telling me to sit down. She explained that her readings cost £25 or £35, depending on what a person was willing to pay; before I committed to handing over any money, I wanted to know the difference between the two types of readings. She clarified by saying that one was just longer than the other. Before having a chance to make my mind up she lunged for the tarot; she whipped out the cards, laid them out in a pattern and proceeded to give me a reading.

This was what I had been looking forward to. I found myself quite eager at the prospect of the things she was about to tell me, but unfortunately ended up flabbergasted and not in a good way. Being flabbergasted was an understatement, because everything she told me was completely wrong. So obviously, what else could I do but complain that nothing she had described was true? Pauline looked a bit flustered, but she persevered and told me two things: that I had a red car and that my mother was in the spirit world. Earlier that day, Mam had been well and truly alive. I didn't complain again, thinking she might need time to warm up before she would begin to get things right. I debated how long to let the reading continue, but eventually put a stop to it before she embarrassed herself any further. Clearly, she wanted to know what was wrong. She wasn't very good at reading people, because she should have picked up the problem from my body language alone.

After enduring Pauline's attempts for twenty minutes, I decided to show her how, from my experience, it should be done. I explained there was a man stood behind her called Mark. She visibly jumped as I continued to tell her that this man had taken his own life, and he had been very close to her. It was quite amusing in a way to turn the tables on Pauline, but her reaction was to drop the cards and her mouth fell wide open.

She also let out a gasp and wanted to know how I knew about Mark. I thought it should have been self-explanatory for a woman in her position to understand, but explained I was a medium trying to develop my skills. I then told her what this man had come to say. The reading began with Mark - Pauline's ex-partner who had hung himself - and ended with information about her mother's health, and her daughter. With that I had succeeded in causing a complete reversal in circumstances; I gave Pauline a proper reading, which she had probably never experienced.

Pauline was dumbstruck; she hadn't expected anything like this to happen to her, but the truth of the matter was that I had been trying to impress her as I fancied a job at the psychic fair. As well, giving readings to lots of different types of people would definitely improve my skills. Hopefully, my little demonstration had made an impact. I plucked up the courage to ask how to get a job here, and who I would have to see. Pauline pointed to a little man with a beard. She called him Sid and nodded at him across the room with a scornful look on her face. She explained that she would still need to charge me for taking up her time, or she would be in big trouble with Sid. So, I decided it would be easier to just pay the money and went to try my luck at getting a job.

◆ ◆ ◆

SID AND THE PSYCHIC FAIRS

Sid was a horrible little man. He was small and quite fat. He wore a tatty waistcoat under his faded suit, the collar of his shirt was frayed and dirty, and he had piercing brown, bloodshot eyes. Cautiously, I went up and told Sid I was after a job; I didn't really like the man much as there wasn't a very good vibe about him, but I did want a job. Sid looked me up and down derisively and wanted to know if I was any good. I told him to ask Pauline what she thought - given I'd just told her a few things - so Sid did just that. She must have given good feedback, as Sid decided to take me on. He told me to start the following week. This was great news - I was so happy and felt over the moon.

The next week I found myself in Scotland full of anticipation for my first Psychic Fair. It was in a fairly big hall and I managed to find a seat behind a rather small table. Pauline was sat on the other side of the room, where she waved at me, and there were another two ladies sat behind tables ready to give readings as well. I'd been given a card which I plonked on the table. It read: *Jimmy Mac Medium and Clairvoyant.* Secretly, I was very proud of this sign and excited about starting this new job. To actually get to this place in Scotland I had to find my own way; there was no such luck as having a coach to take us to the venue, and I had to pay to stay in a hotel. Apparently, expenses weren't included – just a cut of the day's takings. According to Sid, the more readings the mediums did and the quicker they got through people, the more money we would all make.

I didn't like Sid's attitude. As far as I was concerned, the money was a side-issue. All I wanted to do was to help people, but Sid was a businessman and consequently in it for the money; his approach was therefore understandable. If it wasn't for people like Sid organising psychic fairs, the general public probably wouldn't know where to go for a message or to get help.

Thinking about this, I watched Sid in the corner of the room; he was overseeing the proceedings. For a while I sat there expectantly and a little nervous, waiting for the public to enter. I signalled the first person I saw to come over, as I could see from Sid's gesturing that it was time to begin.

My first client was a young Scottish girl that swayed towards my stand. At first, I thought there was something wrong with her, but when she sat down, she absolutely stunk of booze; it was only two o'clock in the afternoon, and that was the reason she wasn't able to walk straight.

In a broad Scottish accent, she slurred something about being desperate and needing a reading. I told her to relax, and explained I'd try to see if anyone would come through for her. Asking my spirit guide to come close, the first thing she needed to hear with a great sense of urgency was that she had to go home now, because her father, James, was worried about her.

At that the girl broke down in tears; she'd had a big falling out with her dad who lived in Glasgow. A lady called Jeannie was her Mother, and she, along with a young boy James – who was possibly her brother - were also desperate for her to return.

The reading continued and a few other things were explained, but the girl seemed overcome with emotion. She'd hoped that her family were missing her and might want her back. She'd been in a pub nearby and noticed the signs for the fair; so, popped in on the spur of the moment, but hadn't expected to get a message that was so direct and straight to the point.

She promptly handed over the payment, and said she had to leave to think about her situation. She left as quickly as she could in her given state. Even though she was quite drunk, the gratitude was visible in her eyes. Even now I wonder whether the girl returned home to her family in Glasgow. Hopefully she did, because it's that sort of reading that makes my job worthwhile. It also means the job's been done right. Readings that touch people like that - make you feel you've affected a person's life in a positive way – and this is something you don't easily forget.

◆ ◆ ◆

There was a lot of message-giving that day, but the next reading that was particularly memorable was for a man who caught my eye while giving other readings. He was an old bald chap, waiting in line. He looked rather like Alfred Hitchcock but smaller. Every time it was this man's turn, he would let someone else go in front of him instead. He was obviously reticent for some reason - or possibly scared – intrigued, I kept watching him and named him Alfred in my head. Eventually the man plucked up the courage and sat down at the table in front of me.

The first thing I asked was if he had ever been to a medium before, to which he explained he'd never had the need before. Some people go regularly and know what to expect, but this man didn't, hence his reluctance to come forward. I told him just to relax and I'd see what we can get; but immediately, before I'd even finished saying the word relax, I could sense the presence of a lady next to me.

She was smaller than the man in front of me. I started to converse with the lady to find out some details before I explained to the client what was happening. Initially, communication began by requesting the lady tell me who she was and why she was here. In a split second of asking the reply came, *'I'm his Mother. I just died a month ago. He looked after me; that's my son – he looked after me well and I love him.'* I asked if she would give her name, and I got the reply *'Mary'*.

So, I proceeded to tell this man all the information received. It hadn't taken long, only a minute. I told him his mother was here and immediately he broke down. The man looked about 65 to 70 years old and I had to wait patiently for him to pull himself together, but the truth was I was also getting a bit tearful. I could feel the love and emotion coming from Mary to her Son but had to wait until the man was ready and able to truly listen.

Eventually, the man received the message that he'd done a marvellous job of looking after his Mother and she was really grateful. She wanted him to know how much she appreciated what he'd done for her because she hadn't really let him know this while she was alive.

Alfred was really pleased. By the end of the reading he looked like he'd had the weight of the world lifted from his shoulders. It transpired that the man thought he hadn't done a good enough job of looking after his Mother, and that was why he had been so restrained in coming forward for a reading. It was lovely that he now knew his mother was absolutely over the moon with how he had cared for her.

At the end I inquired politely as I had been taught. I asked if the reading had been alright, and Alfred replied, looking much happier, that it was wonderful. He went on to explain that he did actually believe in these things, but he'd never had the need to see a medium before. He was really grateful that he had been helped so much more than he thought he would be.

It turned out that the man was a high court-judge, and I was quite surprised as I hadn't expected someone of his standing in the community to visit a medium. However, this added to me being very pleased with how the reading turned out; I was satisfied that I had done a worthwhile job.

♦ ♦ ♦

THE JAM AND BREAD WOMEN

Two women walked over to my table; I could tell they didn't have much money by their appearance. They sat down at the table expectantly. One woman spoke up and asked for a reading. After much deliberation they decided to choose the £25 option. They weren't bothered by how long it would last; they just wanted a message of some kind. However, they were very nervous. Straight away there was a lovely lady from the spirit world stood behind one of the women. I remember telling her that I thought I had her Gran here with me.

Her response greatly amused me; all she could say was, "Oooohh" and she had total disbelief on her face. The lady's name from the spirit world was Betty, and when I told them this, the response from both of them was, "Eeeehhh." "That's right," they said, frantically nodding their heads. But I laughed at their reaction, because I knew it was right, as Betty was stood right there giving me this information. With that the women seemed to become more at ease; they dropped their guard a bit, which makes it easier for me to communicate with the other side.

The more relaxed a person is, the more the energy seems to flow without any blocks (blocks are things such as a person sat there thinking: *'get on with it'* or *'I'm not telling you anything; you should know everything'*). Betty, the lady from the spirit world was laughing her head off, and it was catching as I was also laughing. The woman looked at her friend as if to say, *'why is he laughing at me?'* Then I told her that Betty was showing me one of the ladies as a little girl holding two slices of bread with jam in the middle. It was a jam sandwich the little girl had made, and she was on a flight of stairs walking up with the jam and bread shoved down her knickers. Well, after this the women lost the plot; they were laughing really hard, rolling about on the chairs and said, "you could never have known that in a million, million years." They thought it was, in their words, "Ef'ing marvellous."

I asked if they could understand what I'd just told them and if it was true, but the woman just kept shaking her head and asking how I knew. Again, I explained this information had been given to me by her grandmother, and that she still hadn't finished. Betty was still laughing as she gave details of what actually happened in the story. She explained to me that she was going to bed and took the jam sandwich because she was hungry. Although, once she had gotten into bed and taken the jam sandwich out of her knickers, she heard her father coming up the stairs. Hurriedly she put the sandwich under her pillow, and hoped he wouldn't see it hidden, so as not to get into trouble.

The woman said that the story was absolutely right, but Betty was still talking so I continued. The thing was, when her father had gone back downstairs, there was jam everywhere; all over the pillows and in her hair. The next day she got a good hiding for it. Both her and her friend were falling about laughing and going, "aye, aye that's true," but were still in disbelief about how I could have known. There were some other things that were going to happen in their lives as well, which I described, but I remember that reading so clearly because it was so funny. It's easier to remember the funny ones because they make a nice change to hear - and normally they are few and far between.

◆ ◆ ◆

THE END OF THE PSYCHIC FAIRS

The psychic fairs were good practice, and I had travelled all over the country with mostly enjoyable experiences. However, Sid who was in charge was a very greedy man and a bit of a con-artist. He was supposed to be a Medium, but he never did any work; he kept his eye on everyone else and made sure they pulled their weight so he could make the maximum profit.

If someone wasn't performing by bringing in a certain amount of money, they were soon given the chop and replaced. The other mediums and I had to pay our own petrol and hotel expenses and give Sid half of the cash we earned. So, in the end, the job paid hardly anything at all. The only reason I continued was because of the astonishing variety of experiences I gained doing such a lot of readings every day.

The pace, however, was unrelenting; it soon took its toll. It was really exhausting and an extremely draining part of my life, so when the tour came back to Stockton, I decided to pack the job in.

◆ ◆ ◆

THE PUB CIRCUIT

After finishing the fairs I now found myself living in a pub. Upon spending a few nights in the bar, some of the regulars found out I was psychic and could talk to dead people. They really showed an intense curiosity in the subject, asking all sorts of different questions. At the time, this to me was another opportunity to hone my skills as a medium; so, I approached the owner. A psychic evening, I explained, would be an easy way to answer everyone's questions, and asked if he would be interested. The owner thought this was a great idea because he would be able to make extra money with the interest generated; he began organising it straight away.

The night came and the pub was absolutely crowded. We didn't have any idea it was going to be so popular but knew many people didn't have much knowledge about the other side or what to expect. Again, standing in front of an audience felt quite intimidating, and I was quite nervous to start with. My throat was dry even though I was, laughably, in a pub; the room was full of smoke, warm, and dingy. Clearing my throat, I looked out over the crowd. There was a few who were already quite merry, and some tables that looked quite rowdy and rough, but I was sure I would be able to handle them if they got out of hand. This did feel like quite a bit of pressure because I was stood in front of about 100 slightly intoxicated people, some more than others. With no script and no idea about what to say, I wondered what was going to happen and whether we might have a drunken riot on our hands.

Taking a deep breath, I stood there, surveying the crowd for a few more minutes. I watched the patrons, wondering where to start when the spirit of a man walked through the wall and stopped more or less in front of me. He pointed directly to a lady in the audience. The man had materialised through the wall, but he only had one leg and it was more like he had glided. So, I began, "Do you understand about the chap with one leg who has just walked in?" Well the crowd were in uproar; they fell about laughing, which was probably a lot to do with the drink. When they had quietened down a bit, the lady said, "Yes, that was me Dad," and the evening went on from there. It was a roaring success.

That little start broke the ice nicely; it made me feel calm and once I knew the spirits were there talking to me, it had both me and the crowd far less uptight. Subsequently, when giving more messages, I got the feeling that they would listen to me, rather than try to put me down or heckle me. This was a huge relief. A lot of the time when people think you are genuine and can communicate with spirits, they are frightened to jeer in case you send a spirit home with them to haunt them.

Another message I gave didn't go down quite so well. There was a portly lady in the audience who was being told by her aunt that she was too frivolous; her Aunt was communicating that the lady needed to stop spending so much money. She should also spend less time cavorting with different men and gossiping; it was time for her to settle down. Her aunt obviously didn't approve of her lifestyle, but the lady sat there shaking her head and saying, "no, that's not me; I don't do that." All the rest of her friends on the table were nodding their heads and laughing, mouthing, 'that's exactly what she does.'

I moved on and didn't stop speaking all night; the atmosphere was great, and full of laughter most of the time. This was especially so when I began telling one man the spirit of his Grandad had been watching him decorate his front room. He said he had watched him shorten the legs on a table so he could get it out of the room, instead of just manoeuvring it round the door. Everyone was in stitches with that revelation.

The night continued and there was a real-feel good atmosphere. By the time people came to leave everyone was in a jovial mood; even the owner, as his takings for the night had increased dramatically. Unsurprisingly, many requests to work in lots of different pubs in the area poured in as news travelled fast on the grapevine. People had heard about me and wanted to see me, so I accepted a few invitations. The landlords were pleased because the events brought in a lot of drinking money for them on otherwise quiet nights. This continued for a bit while I lived in the pub, but upon leaving I didn't bother anymore.

♦ ♦ ♦

No matter where I go - whether it's the pub or a friend's house - as soon as people find out I can speak to the other side, they soon become very interested. People tend to be looking over, whispering yet keep their distance; whereas others approach wanting to know more and ask a lot of questions.

I visited a friend, Trevor, and his wife, Becky. It was a sunny afternoon, so we sat in the garden to have a cup of tea. Some other friends of theirs called Liam and

Mandy dropped in. Introductions were made, and the conversation soon turned around to what each of us did. As soon as Mandy heard about my skills, she was full of questions; she didn't really believe in the things I could do and was quite sceptical, but she was like a dog with a bone and wouldn't let the subject drop. Therefore, I decided to tell her what she had been up to in the previous week and described the places she'd been and the things she'd done.

At this, she seemed quite impressed; she wanted to know more about her future, but the understanding being relayed from spirit wasn't good. It was communicated to me that Mandy was to split up with Liam a number of years down the line, although they would still remain friends, and her two children and other family members were going to have health problems. She would also lose her job. There were a lot of other hardships for her to go through as well, but how could I pass any of this information on? It wouldn't help her in the long run; it would worry her, so I said there were no more messages to impart.

However, once Liam and Mandy left, I did tell Trevor and Becky some of the things that were going to happen; I wanted to make sure they could be there when Mandy needed help and support to get through the bad times to come. Trevor always tells me when messages I give come true, and he did tell me all the things passed on about Mandy and Liam had happened over a number of years. I couldn't remember saying them by this time, but it's good to get feedback that the information I give is accurate.

◆ ◆ ◆

UNUSUAL CASES

♦ ♦ ♦

THE SPIRIT IN HIDING

One night, in the middle of summer, the phone rang. I could hear my girlfriend, Vikki, talking, and started listening at the mention of my name. The sentence, "I'm sure Jimmy will sort something out," made me shiver. I pretended to be asleep when she finished the call, hoping she'd leave me alone. For some reason, I just didn't want to hear about the conversation she'd just had. "Jimmy," said Vikki, coming into the room. I snored, but it wasn't very convincing as she gave me a swift kick. I jolted up, and Vikki told me to stop messing about as she wanted to ask me something. *As usual, I thought, someone wants me to do a reading,* but Vikki said it was a bit more complicated than that; so reluctantly I listened.

Vikki's friend Clare had just been on the phone, talking about her friend Jane, who was having problems at home; she felt desperate, not knowing where to turn. Jane's circumstances had changed; she'd recently split from her partner and moved to a new house with her young son of four. Apparently, at first, they loved their new home. Her son, Tim, had his own room and space to play; but, for the last few months, things had changed. Tim had started to scream and cry if he was left alone anywhere in the house. He appeared frightened especially when he was upstairs.

The inexplicable thing was that he had started to get small bruises appearing in places all over his body. Every time Tim was left alone, playing in a room, his mum, Jane, would come back and find him cowering in a corner. Other times, he would suddenly burst into the kitchen - or where ever else she was in the house - crying and upset. When she stayed with him there was no problem and he just played quietly.

♦ ♦ ♦

Jane was at a loss of what to do. She was reaching the end of her tether, as she didn't know how to comfort Tim or understand his unusual behaviour. She'd also begun to notice that objects had moved around in the house, or they seemed to disappear and reappear elsewhere. She thought she was going quite mad until her friend Clare arrived.

It was the first time Clare had visited since Jane had moved in, but as soon as she stepped inside, she could sense something was wrong. She began to experience an unpleasant feeling in the house that she couldn't put her finger on or describe; she simply felt unsettled. She decided to ring Vikki about the strange atmosphere of the house to see if she could get some advice.

A week later, me and Vikki, who was also psychic, found ourselves travelling to Jane's house to see what was going on. It was a big old house in Middlesbrough, and the address was easy to find. We were curious yet not in a rush to get there, as it was a lovely evening and we were enjoying the drive. After a while, Vikki questioned if I was lost; it was a simple route. It was strange but my head felt very foggy, and we appeared to be driving around in circles. The further into the journey, the more unsure I became of which direction we should take.

Vikki kept chirping in with things like, "It's down there isn't it?" It started to get irritating and we were both getting annoyed by our apparent lack of navigation skills. The closer we got to the house, the more we seemed to go wrong. My head was fuzzy; I had brain fog and couldn't concentrate. Not seeming to know where we were, we decided we might as well go back home, thinking we're never going to find the place.

Vikki said her head felt exactly the same, and we both commented it seemed like a clip from *The Exorcist*. We pulled over, where luckily, Vikki retrieved Jane's number and rang for instructions. Once she'd given us the directions, we discovered we were literally around the corner; we recognised the place instantly, as though a veil had been removed from our eyes. This seemed very strange: we'd been scrutinising the names and numbers of the roads and had driven up and down past the very house a number of times. However, I had the distinct feeling that I wasn't wanted there. Luckily, this made me even more determined to sort out whatever was going on.

Vikki knocked on the door. A few moments later Jane appeared with her little boy, Tim, in her arms. "Thank God you've come," she said, tearfully, and ushered us inside. Upon going into the house, I couldn't detect any unpleasantness, or any spirit activity. Jane told us her story again about Tim's bruises appearing all over his body and explained she couldn't understand. When she'd asked Tim about them, he'd say it was the 'bad man.' Whenever he was left alone, he would scream, and shortly afterwards another bruise would appear.

What a strange story, I mused. We decided to start downstairs and took a look around, but there didn't seem to be anything much there. We took the search upstairs, checking the house room by room. We looked in every room but found nothing; no spirits or activity.

There was one room left. *Something must be in here*, I thought, and we entered with trepidation. Again, there was no obvious presence in the bedroom. We knew there must be something going on, but what or where was at a loss to us.

We looked around at the contents of the bedroom. There was Tim's bed and some boxes of toys. Vikki and I stood in the space for a while to get a feel for it. There was a big old wardrobe in the corner, which came into my awareness slowly. Once perceived, I couldn't pull my eyes away from it; they were transfixed.

Next, I started to feel anxious and began sweating. It felt like I was picking up on a spirit's feelings, but at that moment I wasn't in contact with one; it was an odd experience. I wondered whether these feelings were mine and questioned why I would be anxious. I started to move across the room; I was drawn to the wardrobe, but also felt like my feet were glued to the floor. Then we heard it: a long, rattling moan coming from inside the big, heavy wardrobe in the corner of the room.

We both stopped in our tracks. We looked at each other; Vikki's face was a picture. She looked so startled and was rooted to the spot. My limbs were heavy, but I was still able to move and quickly grabbed the door handle. With a bit of a struggle I wrenched the door free, and there inside, trying his best to hide from me, was the spirit of a decrepit old man. He was curled up in a ball, trying to conceal himself in a corner behind some blankets, but soon realised he'd been spotted.

Looking at me scornfully, he uncoiled and rose up. At that moment, I felt what can only be described as a stench of evil flooding from him. Vikki took a sharp intake of breath; she became aware of the spirit's repulsive presence. She felt a chill and began to feel nauseous as the old man stepped from the wardrobe into the room. She couldn't see him, though, as she normally only senses things.

Once he knew he'd been spotted, he began hurling abuse at me. He cursed and swore, almost spitting with venom. The old man moved slowly. He stepped out of the wardrobe, appearing to expand. He was getting bigger and taller, where upon I simultaneously stepped backwards, not wanting to be any closer to the odious spectre. I shouted, "You evil old bastard; you're not staying here!" The spirit of the old man had known we were coming – he'd tried to hide and misdirect us so we wouldn't find him.

Normally, on finding a lost spirit I bless them and help them to cross over. I discerned this spirit wanted desperately to remain here, so my usual method wasn't going to work. This was not going to be simple, so I quickly called for Hawks Wing. He appeared with a knowing look on his face, and without me knowing was already prepared; he had sprung into action and had got help from other entities in the spirit world. As I watched, 12 other spirits - all in hooded gowns which covered and concealed their faces - materialised with Hawks Wing in the small bedroom; they instantly surrounded the old man in a circle.

My mouth fell open. My eyes were wide; I stared at what was happening with tremendous fascination. The old man knew his time here was up; there was nowhere to escape, and he looked petrified. He was making a wild commotion: writhing, cursing, and shouting filthy abuse at Hawks Wing and the others. He was seething at being caught and trying desperately to get away. The spirits moved steadily towards the old man, enclosing the circle.

The spirit of the old man was panicking. He gave the impression he was snarling, while looking frantically around for a way out. One of the hooded spirits seemed to throw something that can only be described as an ethereal blanket over the wicked old man. At the moment the ethereal energy covered the spirit, they all closed in on him, gathering him up. They disappeared silently into a tunnel that had become visible in the corner of the room, taking him away. It was all over in an instant; only Hawks Wing remained.

I breathed a huge sigh of relief and relaxed. I heard Vikki calling my name; she was holding my shoulder and shaking me, wanting to know what had just happened. We both became aware of the changed atmosphere. It felt much lighter and clear, rather like opening a window and letting the smoke out after burning some food. The wide eyed, transfixed look on my face told her something significant had taken place. We went downstairs and sat with Jane; she'd made us a cup of tea, which we sipped while I tried to explain what had transpired. Hawks Wing filled me in on any missing pieces.

◆ ◆ ◆

It turned out the man had actually died in the house. He'd lived there for a long time, and he, as Hawks Wing put it, liked children in a bad way. This, I presumed, meant he had been a paedophile while he was alive. He remained in the house after his death, purely because he was frightened. He had no intention of crossing over because he was too afraid of what was waiting for him on the other side. He was terrified because of the repulsive life he had led, and all the nasty things he'd carried out while he was living.

He'd been watching Tim as he liked young boys; he took every opportunity to prey on him. He had begun to scare and nip Tim whenever he was by himself, as this gave the old man some sort of odd pleasure. Understandably, Tim was petrified of being left alone; especially at night, when he would wake up crying due to being tormented by the old man. However, it was now his time to be dealt with, and we explained what had happened to Jane. She thought Tim was having night terrors; she'd been baffled by all the bruises, but now things started to fall into place and make sense. She looked hopeful, but not quite ready to believe it could all be over.

Vikki and I also realised it must've been the old man giving us brain fog - he knew we were coming and didn't want us to find him. He obviously understood what was going on, as he had been watching the family; he could hear conversations and had probably heard Jane's phone call asking for help. The old man seemed quite sneaky and crafty; and these were probably skills he had practiced during his life as a paedophile.

He had been dead a long while. He seemed to have been honing and increasing his abilities and skills, making him more powerful. He probably enjoyed terrorising all the people who had moved into the rented house over the years. A few weeks later, Jane got in touch. She was much happier; things were back to normal, and nothing else bad had happened. Tim was now able to play by himself in the house without any incidents. His bruises had disappeared, and he had returned to being a normal, happy little boy.

♦ ♦ ♦

THE ATTACHMENT

Another type of spirit in hiding occurred one evening at a development circle. My friend Paul, who is also a medium, ran this development circle above a hairdresser in Stockton; there he taught budding psychics and healers how to progress. He invited me along one night to help him out, and when I got there a number of people had already arrived. They were stood chatting, and I was hanging around in the background when another member of the group entered the room. As soon as she walked in, I could see there was something attached to her energy. I pointed at it and shouted, "get out now." It saw me and I said, "yes you; get out now." Paul had also seen it and was watching, but the thing that was attached to her left quite quickly once it was spotted.

In looking around the room, I saw everybody's faces were in shock. They were all stood with their mouths wide open and eyes popping; especially Sue, the lady who everyone thought I was pointing and shouting at.

When I saw how dumbstruck they all were I apologised and began to explain what had happened.

When someone is very low, which Sue was, they can sometimes get entities which attach to them, draining their energy even further. This is not very common, but it had happened to Sue. She had been very busy at work and at home, looking after her mother, without having any time to relax; but she could feel her energy being drained, and for some reason she was extremely tired. She had been through periods like this before in her life without feeling this way and thought it must be her age. However, since the spirits departure she began feeling a lot lighter, like a weight had been lifted from her. Sure enough, in the coming weeks she reported that she was much better, with a lot more energy.

♦ ♦ ♦

THE SPIRIT AND HIS LADY LOVE

It may seem that my life is full of scary or anxious events; however, my knowledge of spirit has grown over the years and I am stronger and more resilient as a result. With the help of my guides and other spiritual people, I understand a lot more about spirits and the other side. Some mediums haven't had enough experience to gain this knowledge or understanding, and act differently to me in various situations. A case in point was once when I went for a job at a big old local hall, where psychic evenings and ghost hunting was available for anyone. On the Ghost Walk events, people were taken on a tour around the hall and its grounds. The history of the house was described as well as the haunting of any spirits that persisted.

The people running the event asked me to do a trial run; I thought this sounded interesting, so I took part one evening with the tour. So, at ten o'clock at night I pulled up at the historic house. It was dark and I wondered if anyone would attend. Surprisingly, there was a group of about twelve people of differing ages; they had all paid a set fee in order to experience something paranormal. There were some geeky types who looked like they belonged in *Ghostbusters* the movie, and a few who just wanted some fun or a bit of a scare. There was a tour guide dressed in old fashioned black clothes to take the group around and give details about the history of the place. I was there as an extra to pick up on anything supernatural or any actual hauntings. We toured the hall, where the history of the house and anything significant that had occurred was described; the various spectres that people had seen or experienced were linked to these times gone by.

People often say that really old places are probably haunted, but it is rare to pick up on an actual haunting. However, I trudged round with the group, listening to the stories being portrayed, and actually found it quite interesting. We ventured into a corridor, and then a type of lane leading from the main house to the stables. It was here I saw the first spirit I'd picked up on in the place. Apparently, the tour guide was explaining, this was a place with a story about a couple in love who were going to run away together; but due to unforeseen circumstances, the man was killed. This is where I stepped in and stopped the tour guide so I could describe what was happening.

I began to explain that there was a spirit of a gentleman and could sense the spirit was anxious and agitated. He was dressed in a really old-fashioned white shirt over tight trousers and was from around sometime in the 1700s. As I said, he was in quite an agitated state, and said he was there to meet his lady love. She was a kitchen maid and he was a stable lad, and she hadn't shown up. On the night of the rendezvous he was there waiting, when in the meantime the house was attacked, and he must have been killed. Since then, every night for over 250 years or more, he had turned up to meet his love.

The depth of emotion coming from this spirit was so powerful I found myself in tears; I could hardly speak, and tears were streaming down my face. This poor spirit had been feeling this misery for over 250 years since the night of his death. He was still there, waiting at the meeting point to join the love of his life and run away, but she would never arrive. What else could be done but to send him on his way; I couldn't leave him there to repeat that same fateful night over and over again. I blessed him and told him to walk into the light where he would find his lady love. As this was explained to the spirit, a beautiful light appeared close to him; a smile slowly spread across his face. As he disappeared into the light, I could feel immense happiness and joy emerge.

None of the previous mediums on the ghost walk had chosen to move this tormented spirit to the other side. I couldn't believe they had left him there to experience such despair every night. Perhaps they just hadn't spotted him. Through the tears, I explained to everyone on the tour what was happening to the spirit as he was helped, at long last, on his way to complete his final journey.

The people on the ghost walk loved the experience; they really felt part of something significant, giving great feedback about me and the ghostly encounter. However, the organisers weren't very happy that I had managed to get rid of one of their ghosts, so the tour operator said they didn't want me to come back. They wouldn't consider me for a job because they couldn't have me getting rid of all the spirit attractions by sending them on their way. Other mediums may have been happy to leave that poor spirit relive his anguish night after night, but I couldn't.

◆ ◆ ◆

THE WAITING SPIRIT

One day I was out for a walk with a friend, Joe. We chose to visit the beach at Saltburn, which, as previously explained, is a place full of happy times and memories. It was a pleasant evening, and, unusually, there was hardly another person in sight. We talked as we picked our way around rock pools, seaweed and boulders below a steep, high cliff overlooking the beach. There we sat on a boulder, looking out to sea and chatting. In the distance we could see a man with a bucket collecting winkles. He kept looking over in our direction and began making his way towards us, eventually coming very close; almost next to us, still looking for winkles, he asked what we were doing.

Why this man came up and asked two complete strangers on a desolate beach what they were doing I have no idea; but I had been followed by a spirit for a couple of days, and immediately, when the stranger spoke to me, the spirit made himself known. He was actually the father of the winkle picker! So, I began telling this man his father was here and gave him some messages. The winkle man explained he had felt a compulsion to come and join us, and even though he felt a bit pushy he couldn't suppress the urge. By the end of our chance meeting he was overcome with emotion and gratitude; he was very teary eyed. He also happened to be not in the best of health, so I gave him some healing. The man knelt on the beach and I put my hands on his head and channelled healing energy. When we had finished, the man walked away a lot happier and more at ease with life.

This encounter brings up many questions. Are spirits actually powerful enough to engineer chance meetings, or is it that they know in advance what people are going to do in their lives? Was this why a complete stranger was drawn to walk about a mile over an almost deserted beach to strike up a conversation with two men he didn't know? Consider other questions such as: is our life mapped out for us; can spirits see the future; does time exist as we know it or is time different once we pass over?

There are many more questions to ponder; perhaps I'll find out more information from further communication with the spirit world, and from my friends and family who have passed. Every medium seems to have a different piece of the puzzle of the afterlife, but no one seems to understand the whole picture. The thing I realise from all the messages I've received is that love is of paramount importance, and we should try and treat every situation or individual we meet in a loving way. Hopefully this book will inspire people to think more deeply about life, death and the way we act while we are here; so, we're able to follow our life journeys in the best way possible.

◆ ◆ ◆

Printed by Amazon Italia Logistica S.r.l.
Torrazza Piemonte (TO), Italy